How To

Achieve Finical Freedom, Success, and Prosperity. Quit the 9 to 5. Work 4 Hours a Week. Obtain Wealth and Money. Create Over 7 Highly Effective Habits to Do All of This

Jeremy Clark

Disclaimer Notice:

Please note the information contained within this document is for educational and entertainment purposes only. All effort has been executed to present accurate, up to date, and reliable, complete information. No warranties of any kind are declared or implied. Readers acknowledge that the author is not engaging in the rendering of legal, financial, medical or professional advice. The content within this book has been derived from various sources. Please consult a licensed professional before attempting any techniques outlined in this book.

By reading this document, the reader agrees that under no circumstances is the author responsible for any losses, direct or indirect, which are incurred as a result of the use of information contained within this document, including, but not limited to, — errors, omissions, or inaccuracies.

Contents

HOW TO

ACHIEVE FINICAL
FREEDOM, SUCCESS,
AND PROSPERITY.
QUIT THE 9 TO 5.
WORK 4 HOURS A WEEK.
OBTAIN WEALTH AND MONEY.
CREATE OVER 7 HIGHLY EFFECTIVE
HABITS TO DO ALL OF THIS

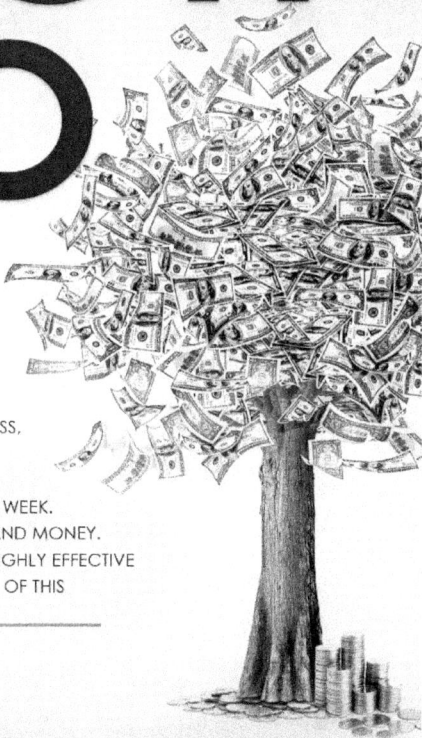

JEREMY CLARK

Chapter 1:
Habits

We all desire the best things in life—we want to have better financial status, form healthy relationships, live healthy lifestyle, and accomplish those goals that we've set for ourselves. Heck! These desires—or should I say, thirsts—are the main reason why we keep trying. It is the reason why we all study frequently, go to work, and why we build relationships. We want to spend our retirement days in a dream house with no outstanding mortgage payments, visit any choice vacation destination, and secure the future of our loved ones. Sadly, not everyone gets to accomplish that dream. For many of us, these dreams and desires get shrouded up in the frustrations and forgotten in the course of our life. Then, we ask ourselves, "what am I doing wrong?" whenever we have a brief awakening. We see others taking giant strides with perceived ease toward their goals. Our social media feeds are filled with these people's accomplishments; from posting about their new house to posting pictures about their exotic vacations. "Life just seems easy for these set of people," we say to ourselves. Unconsciously, we tend to sink back into ourselves and strengthen our old habits. Hold on! Did I mention "habits"? Yes, habits are the reason why success, wealth, and money have become an illusion to so many people. More so, it is the reason why some people are so successful at what they do. Let's look at why habits are so crucial to our dreams, goals, and personal development.

Why Habits Are Important

We all want a better future for ourselves. However, we often fail to regard the one thing that can bring this future to reality: our habits. Every action you take, no matter how small, can kickstart a chain reaction throughout your life. Yes, we forget that our habits can either make or mark us. A simple decision to exercise for 30 minutes a day can improve your health and influence what you're eating.

What's more? Cultivating the habit of having a family dinner can impact the psychological growth of your kids and boost your relationship with your partner. Smoking a cigarette every day can hurt your lungs and overall health. Yes, our life outcome is a result of our habits. Sadly, we all underestimate the power of our habits. We rarely pay attention to actions. Even when we do focus on our actions, we tend to overlook the inane and small ones. We convince ourselves many times that success requires a grandiose action. Whether it involves losing weight, winning a business deal or writing a book, we put pressure on ourselves to make an earth-shattering improvement that will make us famous.

Well, You Are Wrong.

The small habits matter. How? Let's observe the rule of compound interest in finance. Say you save $100 in an investment account with an interest rate of 10% per year; you will get an additional $10 on your initial deposit of $100 after one year. Now, you have $110. The subsequent interest payment will be 10%of your total sum, which is now $121. By the 5th year, your total amount would be approximately $193. This interest keeps compounding until you end up with a huge sum when you want to withdraw.

Small habits work in that same manner. Let's say you decide to invest 5 minutes of your time to exercise. It is impossible for you to notice any new change during the first few days. You may not see a change in the first few days of the second week of your newfound habit; you will only notice a slight change in the first three weeks. During this early phase of your new habit, it is easy to get discouraged since the effects are slow. I refer to this phase as the lag phase. It is the time when most people are tempted to slide back into old habits. If you, however, persist in your actions, the changes will slowly compound until it gains momentum, and this is the time other people will notice the change in you.

Conversely, a few negative habits can stall your growth and self-development. A few extra hours more in front of a TV; a few more hours to nap; and a few soft drinks can compound into an unhealthy lifestyle. Consequently, these unhealthy changes can either result in depression due to your inability to fulfill your goals, or it could result in a plethora of health complications.

That said, your success is not dependent on once-in-a-lifetime achievements; it relies on your ability to adhere to the positive habits in your daily activities. More so, if you want to predict the trajectory of your life, take a moment to observe the little positive and negative habits in you. Remember, time is the multiplier, and it will multiply whatever you invest in it.

Why It's Difficult to Adopt New Habits

Most of us are familiar with the success stories of a lot of popular figures. We know that Warren Buffet, the investment guru, started investment at an early age. What's more? Some are familiar with the story of how Thomas Edison was able to invent the light bulb after a myriad of trials. I know you can recollect word-for-word these success stories from books, TVs, and even the internet. There are so many books about success and the success stories of famous people; these books offer us a glimpse into the lives, habits, and strategies of those who are successful in their respective niche. Despite the wealth of information, we glean from these success stories and often find it difficult to adopt these same positive habits. More so, we find it difficult to break our habits to make room for new ones to grow. Bad habits are like oak trees that have taken time to entrench themselves into your core. Therefore, you need to find a way to uproot these habits, and this requires targeting keynote or foundational habits.

Cast Away the Chains of Procrastination

Procrastination is a keynote habit you must break if you want to achieve your dream. According to Brian Tracy, the author of Eat That Frog, procrastination is the thief of time. It gradually lets you postpone important things until it's nearly too late for you to take charge or complete the task. Procrastination lies as one of the roots of all our bad habits. By procrastinating on curbing unhealthy eating habits or exercising, you are inadvertently compounding your health issues. By procrastinating on a business deal or investment, you are unconsciously drawing nearer to financial ruin. Let me ask you this question: how many times have you procrastinated on a task only to never do it again? It might be a quick errand or a simple task, such as flossing or airing the sheets. It is easier to procrastinate on tasks we perceive as unimportant, and this subsequently leads to failure.

The Illusion of Overnight Success

Just as you must break the chains of procrastination, you need to wake up from the illusions of overnight success. This illusion is sold by the media, your social media feeds, and con men. These outlets focus on the grandiose moments of an individual's accomplishments without care for the years of struggles, pain, discipline, and disappointment before they could achieve that dream. Sadly, some people are swayed by these grandeur moments. Also, we throw away our inhibitions and run after these illusions painted by the media. So, let me set the facts straight: there's no shortcut to achieving your dreams. Just as a child must crawl before it can walk and later talk, growth and development are in sequential order, and there's no alternative to this process. You must put in the hard work and persist even when the odds are no longer on your side. Funny enough, the logical part of your brain understands that the process of growth cannot be skipped. However, the emotional part of the brain finds it difficult to comprehend the concept.

Consequently, we could opt for quick ways to bypass the long process of growth and development. It is the reason why we easily fall into get-rich-quick schemes. Thomas Edison didn't become a well-recognized figure overnight; he reportedly failed so many times before he could invent the light bulb. Mahatma Karamchand Gandhi didn't achieve his dream for independence overnight; he went on numerous hunger strikes, walked for miles, and suffered a lot of persecutions before he achieved his breakthrough. So, look beyond the illusion of overnight success and peer into the backstage to get a glimpse of to achieve that change.

How to Create Long-Term Changes?

We adopt new habits because we desire to create lasting change in an area of our life. However, it's disappointing when we fail to adhere to these new habits due to a busy schedule or family emergencies or any other circumstances. Most times, we fail to adhere to these new habits because our reasons are weak. Therefore, I will show you how to adhere to these habits by incorporating the three main principles of change into your daily activities. But hold on! Before we delve into these principles, I want to explore the importance of a paradigm shift and how it can help you to create lasting change.

Understanding Paradigm Shifts

Your paradigm or perception is the way you view the world. Surprising as it might seem, the way you view the world determines your success. It determines your good or bad habits. Just a slight shift in your perception can set the groundwork for your newfound habits. To understand this concept better, let's think of paradigms, or perceptions, like a map. The concept of paradigm is like maps. Just like maps, you will arrive at your destination if you have the right perception. Alternatively, having the wrong perception is just like having the wrong map: you will never arrive at your destination. You might have the right attitude or work faster and diligently, but you will still be lost if you have the wrong perception.

How Do We Form Paradigm Shifts?

Everyone has a literal map or perception in their head. Sometimes, these perceptions are based on reality, while some are based on values or the way we think things should be. These maps or perception becomes the lens through which we view and interpret all our experiences. We seldom question the accuracy of our perceptions. Heck! We rarely even notice their existence. We assume that things are the way we see them. More so, our attitudes and behaviors stem from these assumptions. Therefore, when we open our mouth to describe the things we see, we are inadvertently describing ourselves, our paradigms, and perceptions.

Why Some Never Have A Paradigm Shift

Most times, we are intrigued by the success and accomplishment of others. We admire their principles, teamwork, strength, maturity, and family bond. Some, however, take it a step further by requesting for the secret of their happiness, success, and techniques. Sadly, most of those who make this appeal are looking for a quick fix. Even taught these skills, they never really understand the depth and eventually lose it. It's the reason why some are rooted in the same position, despite reading a myriad of motivational books. Why? Because they are looking for a quick solution to their life issues without attacking the underlying problem of their stagnation.

The Power of an "Aha Moment"

Do you see the light bulb that shines above a cartoon character when it has an idea? Well, this is what happens when you have a paradigm shift or an "Aha Moment." This moment is what you experience when you start to see the world in a different light. It's a rare dose of epiphany that some people might not experience in their lifetime. At that moment, you become awed by the magnitude of another perception and how much you've missed out. Archimedes, a Greek mathematician, was able to create the floatation principle that is widely used in various aspects of engineering. His "Aha Moment" occurred when he went to take a soak at the public bath. He noticed that his body displaced part of the water in the tub as he stepped in it and that was the moment, he had his epiphany. So many prominent people today were able to create lasting habits through a paradigm brought about by an "Aha Moment."

Mind you, having a paradigm shift is not limited to an "Aha Moment." Sometimes, you get a paradigm shift in the face of life-altering experiences such as the death of a loved one, or at the top of taking a drastic step. Furthermore, your paradigm shift can come slowly as a result of a series of events that changed your perception.

THE THREE MAIN PRINCIPLES OF CREATING LASTING CHANGE

Raise Your Standards

It is sad that we underestimate our capabilities and demand so little of ourselves. Therefore, if you want to stand shoulder-to-shoulder with the giants you so much adore, you need to raise your standards. It's that straightforward. Write down the things you will no longer tolerate in your life and all the things you aspire to become. Put it up on the door of your room and your refrigerator. If, however, you find yourself doubting your capabilities, look at the lives of those who have made their marks in the world. From Martin Luther King Jr. to Rosa Parks, to Mahatma Gandhi, to Abraham Lincoln; these people changed the status quo, and history will never forget their impact.

Build Your Conviction

It is not enough to raise your standards if you don't believe in what you are doing. You had already sabotaged yourself before you started the habit. It's no surprise that many people are unable to follow a habit since they don't believe in the long-term benefit. Your convictions are like unquestioned orders, telling us what's possible and what's not possible, telling of how things are, and what we can do or not. They shape our actions, thoughts, and every emotion that we pass through. Therefore, building your conviction can raise your confidence and boost the confidence of those around you. Mind you, I'm not saying the process will be easy, but you can build your conviction via the following steps:

- Stop the negative talk: Never, I repeat, never practice self-criticism. Yes, we are our worst critics, but you should try to start trusting yourself and what you are saying. More so, avoid those who will sap your self-esteem with destructive criticism and negative talk.

- Reflect on your past achievement: It is easy to get weighed down by present circumstances. Therefore, try to reflect on what you have internally (self-worth; values; beliefs; love; compassion; confidence; happiness; experience; relationship; self-respect). Also, you can reflect on what you have externally (family; friends; career and business).

- Lastly, develop your convictions until you are firmly rooted in your beliefs. Remember, don't think about what others think of you, as this might be a stumbling block to your progress.

Change Your Strategy

When you raise your standards and build your convictions, I believe it's time to figure out a strategy to accomplish your goals. You have your goals in mind; you want to shed off some pounds; you want to have a million dollars at the end of a set duration. The next thing is for you to plan strategies to make your goals come to life. For you to accomplish this, you need to gain control over the five main aspects of your life: emotions, relationship, finance, time, and health.

Gain Control Over Your Emotions

Every action we take is basically to change the way we feel. For instance, you lose some extra pounds because you want to feel positive and confident about your body. Yes, we let our emotions drive our goals, and thus lead to various implications. When you depend on your emotions to make certain life-altering decisions, you will certainly make lots of mistakes. Failing to take control of your emotions can leave you at the mercy of outside elements.

Furthermore, you will never achieve your goals. Therefore, learning to control your emotions is an effective strategy to change your life. This time, you need to identify your overpowering emotions and how to use them to your advantage.

Gain Control Over Your Physical Health

You can never enjoy your accomplishments if you are riddled with poor health. It translates to failure if you ignore your health while building other aspects of your life. Learning to gain control over your physical health will help you to control your eating habits. Furthermore, it will help you to always go for medical check-ups. Remember, when you have good health that you can chase your goals.

Gain Control Over Your Relationships

Personally, there's nothing I can think of as important as gaining control over your relationships—family, business, social, and business. Gaining control over your relationships is a good strategy for creating lasting change. So, start by discovering what you value most, your expectations, your rules in the game of life, and how it relates to those around you. When you relate with those around you, you will be rewarded with a sense of contribution. More so, it will give the feeling that you've made a difference in other people's lives.

Gain Control Over Your Finances

According to recent studies, most American senior citizens are in financial constraints. Sadly, none of these people planned for this type of future as they worked toward their retirement. Therefore, you need to gain control of your finances right now irrespective of your age, status, or race. First, change the belief that money is the solution to an easier life or happiness. Rather, I want you to gain control of your finances, irrespective of the amount you have with you. The only way you can achieve this is by adopting new habits that will help you save toward your financial dreams. Let go of unnecessary expenses and build a future for yourself.

Gain Control Over Time

Time is not your friend. Time waits for no one. These are the basic misconception about money that we hear every day. Let me ask you a question: do you know how to use time? Permit me to change your belief right now: time is what you make of it. Let me explain further: if you decide to waste your time on instant gratification, then time will never be enough for you to chase your dreams. However, if you decide to manage your desires for instant gratification and allow your dreams and creations to grow, then time will become your ally. Once you finally gain control over time, you will find out that you can achieve so much within even a few days!

Chapter 2:
Start Your Day Right

We wake up every day to a plethora of tasks with varying magnitude and difficulty. Sometimes, we get discouraged to even start at all due to the enormity of what we must do. Why? It's because our mind automatically focuses on the big tasks while shifting the small tasks to the bottom of the list. We think if we can complete the big tasks, then we'll have enough time and motivation to jump on the less important ones. However, we find ourselves completely exhausted physically and emotionally after completing the bigger tasks. Sadly, we never get around to doing it until it overwhelms us. Little tasks such as making the bed can overwhelm you when done at the wrong time. In this chapter, we will look at the importance of each small task on our goals and dreams. Furthermore, we will examine the common misconception of completing small tasks, how to find your productive hours, and how you can establish your foundation habits. Before we do, let's discuss the bed-laying principle.

The Bed-Laying Principle
Admiral William H. McRaven, an alumnus of the University of Texas, was the keynote speaker at the University's 2014 graduation

ceremony. In a hall brimming with graduates eager for a taste of the outside world, the Admiral was able to deliver a stunning speech which, I believe, made an indelible mark on those present. After a brief introduction about his entry into a navy school, McRaven talked about the inspection procedure of his instructors at the academy. The instructors, who were veterans from the Vietnam War, would parade down the halls and inspect the recruit's beds. McRaven noted that no matter how much they laid their beds; the instructors just weren't satisfied. I find it surprising that these war veterans could focus on a small and inane task as bed laying. Could there be something more attached to it?

As if he could read my thought, the Admiral laid bare the bed-laying principle. He said start your day by changing the bed if you want to conquer the world. Laying your bed is an activity that counts as a small win and gives you the needed euphoria to take on huge tasks later in the day.

He also pointed out the fact that how are you going to complete the big tasks if you can't handle the small ones.

It Starts with The Small Wins

Just as Admiral McRaven graciously pointed out, simple habits or actions such as laying the bed are small wins that eventually give you the motivation to take on huge tasks. Various researches allude to the fact that these small or inconsequential actions can fuel transformative changes that become a pattern. Furthermore, the patterns formed convince you that bigger achievements are within reach. For instance, deciding to drink a glass of juice every morning can create a pattern for a healthy lifestyle.

What's more? This small habit will gradually become a pattern, and consequently, give you the energy to take on a huge task. However, not all small tasks are worth investing in. Some folks make the mistake of investing in small actions that have no positive impact on their ability to tackle huge tasks. For instance, small actions such as leaving dirty dishes in the sick to dedicate a few minutes to appreciate your loved ones can eventually become a pattern which will strengthen your relationships. Taking a minute to appreciate people will make you feel happy about yourself. And that is the reaction/emotion which will provide you with the needed motivation to tackle any task head-on.

Wait!

Before you jump on the bandwagon of doing any small habit, I want you first to identify the ones that will have a positive impact on you. What's more? I want you to select small habits that will kickstart a chain reaction of productivity in your life. Yes, there's a name for these types of habits, and they are referred to as keystone or foundation habits.

Harnessing the Power of Keystone Habits

According to the bed-laying principle, some tasks have the potential to start a chain reaction, thereby influencing other tasks in your schedule. A simple task such as washing the dishes or vacuuming under the chairs can spur you to go on a cleaning spree in other parts of your house. With time, these minor tasks become habits or patterns which gradually seep into other areas. The power of keystone habits lies in the realization that you can get everything right; that you can't complete all the tasks in your schedule. More so, it lies in the ability to identify a few important priorities and fashioning them into powerful levers. I recommend starting with a small task with the potential of becoming a keystone habit. These tasks, however minute, will have the ability to shift and remake other habits. Here's an example to help you understand better. Paul wants to lose a few extra pounds to complete his company's annual marathon event. Since he became the vice president, there's no alternative for him; he must compete. The event is still three months away and every passing day fills him with the trepidation of losing. Rather than tremble at the thought of embarrassing himself on the D-day, Paul decided to act. He would wake up every morning by 5 a.m. to jog for 30 minutes. Paul thought he was going to die on the first day. The first few days were hell for him. However, the second and third week weren't that bad. With time, Paul noticed he had stopped eating more and become more conscious with his diet. Interestingly, he's more productive in his workplace. He has developed a great relationship with his colleagues. What's more? His family can't get enough of him. Now, what you think caused this chain reaction in Paul's life? The answer, my dear reader, lies in the power of keystone habits.

Here's another thought-provoking question: Why is it so difficult to adopt this concept since it seems so simple and easy? Well, the answer is not far-fetched. Heck! You might have said it yourself or heard it from those around you. Are you curious to know? Then, let's jump into the next section.

Statement 1: "I Don't Feel Motivated"

No doubt, this is one of the good old statements we use as an excuse when we fail to follow up on new habits. Don't deny it: we are all guilty of this at times. For example, we decide to change our lives, so we set a major goal and try to build habits to help us achieve our targets. We succeed for a few days until life throws a wrench into our newfound habits, thereby skipping a day. Sadly, the pattern repeats itself. We try again with a burning desire to push through irrespective of any circumstance. Once again, we miss a day or two dues to another circumstance which could be our old habits or external forces. Eventually, you quit in frustration and conclude that this is not for you. Do you want to know the truth? It's not easy building new habits, especially keynote habits. I'm sure many experts will tell you to cultivate a new habit by doing it daily. Yes, it's so easy to say those words or read them in a book. However, it is most difficult to see it through. Why? Because we live hectic lives, so it's difficult to try anything consistently. More so, it is challenging to add an extra task to your already tight and hectic schedule.

Motivation Is Not Enough; You Need Willpower

As you progress through life, you will realize that motivation is not enough—it's just the tip of the iceberg. Do you want to know what's beneath the iceberg? It's your willpower. Sure, you can listen to inspiring motivation talks or read books on success to get energized. However, motivation won't get you through the times when you're feeling tired and disenchanted about working on a task. Yes, this is the time when you need your willpower. Besides the possessing conscience, self-awareness, and imagination, your willpower is your fourth human endowment. It empowers your self-management strategies. It's the ability to make choices and decisions and act by them. The human willpower is an amazing concept that has helped so many people to surmount different situations. For examples, various studies prove that students with strong willpower had excellent grades compared to those without. These students spent less time in front of the TV or any distractions. Sadly, not everyone possesses strong willpower. Just like a muscle, you need to exercise your willpower continuously until it becomes strong enough to help you push through dire circumstances. So, how will you build your willpower? By practicing self-discipline. Self-discipline is derived from disciple, which means your ability to follow or stick to philosophy or habit. You need to stick to your small task's day-in and day-out until your willpower is strong enough.

Statement 2: "I Can't Remember to Complete the Small Tasks"

Here comes another common statement. This type of statement makes me ponder on the reasons why people fail to complete small tasks. After studying and interacting with so many people, I've come to one conclusion: the difficulty in completing small tasks is related to a concept called cognitive load.

Let me elaborate.

The human brain has a short-term memory and a long-term memory. We depend on our short-term memory when we try to accomplish and incorporate new habits. Sadly, the human brain can only store about seven chunks of information in its short-term memory. Since only a tiny fraction of what we know is stored in our working memory, we often depend on our long-term memory and habits to accomplish almost every task in life. For example, when you first learned how to drive a car, you had to put in a conscious effort to carry out the process for each action. This included tasks like parallel parking, changing lanes, driving with a stick shift, or using a turn signal. In the beginning, each of these tasks required a constant reinforcement of your short-term memory until it becomes a habit that does not require much thought process (long-term memory). More so, when it becomes a habit, it frees your mind to focus on other tasks, such as an off-key version to your favorite playlist.

Let's use a different example to demonstrate your cognitive load. Small habits such as tracking your expenses or doing your tax calculations are the key to gaining control over your finances. It is not hard to perform these tasks because they only require a few minutes to complete. However, it is also easy to forget because it's not an automatic component of our daily routine. Therefore, if you don't use a "trigger" to remind you of these small tasks, then it will be difficult for tracking your expenses daily. This is also the reason why it's easy to consistently perform simple tasks, such as brushing your teeth or bathing. Why? It is because you know the negative consequences of not brushing your teeth, and this acts as a trigger to spur you on.

Another reason why people often remember to perform consistent small tasks such as brushing the teeth is that it's attached to a larger routine that you complete when you wake in the morning. Therefore, brushing your teeth is an automatic action since it doesn't strain your cognitive load.

How Can You Adopt New Tasks?

So, how can you integrate new small tasks into your long-term memory to become automatic? Well, you have already discovered the answer yourself. You need to anchor or attach your new habits to an existing routine; or better yet, set a timer that notifies you of your tasks every day. There are myriads of ways with which you can carry out the small tasks in your routine.

Build A Priority List

Yes, it's that simple. Build a list of all your important activities and start with the small tasks at the top and the big tasks at the bottom. Arrange your small tasks and big tasks in order of importance or urgency. While making this list, you will realize that not all tasks are urgent or important. Furthermore, some task requires just a few minutes and little-expended energy, while others might gulp all your time and energy. So, I'll advise you to start with the ones that require less energy and less time before attempting the more tasking ones.

Declutter Your Daily Schedule

Why do you have to wear yourself out by attempting so many tasks in a day? Doing this will not only wear you out but fill you with a sense of accomplishment. In such a scenario, I want you to sieve through myriads of daily activities and select the ones with the potential to create a positive impact. Be realistic: you are not helping anyone if you wear yourself out. It might even affect your productivity for the next day.

No doubt, we often forget about the importance of each day in how our lives turn out. It is possible to overlook the little actions and big actions that sum up our day.

Chapter 3:
Life is Unfair, Get Over It

Life is unfair. Life is unfair to the employee who worked so much for a promotion but was bypassed due to his/her gender. Yes, it is unfair to the child born with cystic fibrosis, who might never have a fair chance at life. Let's not forget the war veteran who must live on scraps despite going on several tours for his country. Life is unfair to the woman who had to suffer emotional abuse at the hands of her loved one. Have you forgotten about life's unfairness to a student who was denied a scholarship based on the color of his skin, despite exceeding the requirements? What about the child who had to grow up in an abusive environment? Do you want to know the truth? Life is unfair to everyone. No matter what, life will never give you only rainbows and unicorns; you will also get to taste the wrong side of life. Everywhere you go, you see people blaming their loved ones, their friends, their country, even the world. Do you want the bigger truth? Life is what you make of it. Perhaps, you think you have the worst situation in the world, and no one can ever grasp the depth of your situation. Well, here's an example to show you someone who had it worse.

Life Is What You Make of It

Jake and Mark are twin brothers. They lived in the makeshift home made from wood and pieces of cardboard to shut out the elements. All their lives, they've neither felt the warm embrace of their parents nor do they know affection. They lost their parents and elder siblings at an early age to the greedy hands of death due to an epidemic that swept across the village. Life was difficult for these twins in an area with little-to-no resources. They had to scrounge from the leftover bones at the butcher shops and rummage through the refuse heaps to find a few good vegetables. No one ever thought to lend a helping hand. Why? The villagers all felt they were unfortunate and didn't want their aura to cross their doorstep. No one wanted them around, even little kids who are often known to have no fear of strangers, steered clear of the twins. Life would, however, offer them a reprieve in the form of a vacancy for workers on a construction site. Now, let's fast forward to the future: Jake is married with three beautiful kids and a happy and healthy circle of friends. Also, he's the regional manager of a large store in the city. Mark, however, is a chronic alcoholic, drug addict, and financially broke. He's back in the makeshift home of his childhood. Interestingly, both men turned out differently despite growing up in the same restrictive environment.

Let me ask you: what could have gone wrong?

Perhaps, we should ask both men the reason why they are in their present predicament?

Do you know what they will say?

Interestingly, both men would say, "What could I have become, having grown up in that deplorable condition." Well, they couldn't have been far from the truth. So many times, we have been seduced to think that our environment shaped us the way we are, and events control our thoughts. And this is the greatest lie of all because life is what we make of it. If you believe that you are a victim of your circumstances, then you become a victim. On the other hand, if you believe that you can make the best of your life despite the glaring disadvantage you've been served, then you will achieve your goals. Our beliefs, rather than our circumstances, have the power to shape us.

What Is Belief?

It is necessary for us to start with a simple introduction before I explore the complex aspects of how beliefs influence our perception of the world. So, what are beliefs, anyway? Beliefs are feelings of certainty about something. For instance, if you believe that you are beautiful, what you are trying to say is, "I'm certain I'm beautiful." That sense of certainty allows you to tap into innate resources that prove you are beautiful - it's that simple. Interestingly, we all have the potential for virtually anything. However, we limit ourselves via our lack of certainty in belief.

Here's another way to understand the concept of beliefs: beliefs are made up of tiny building blocks called ideas. There are lots of ideas running through your head right now. However, you don't believe all of them. An idea can only become a belief when you are certain of its authenticity via your inner convictions or from external forces. Here's a way to differentiate a belief from an idea. Stop for a few minutes and say to yourself, "I'm brave." Now, how certain do you feel about that statement? Well, if you think, "perhaps, I'm not brave," you are not certain of your courage.

Alternatively, if you believe that you are brave, then you might experience some references from those around you. For instance, people may have commended you quite a lot about your braveness. However, all these commendations mean nothing until you have solidified the belief in your heart.

Beliefs Are Formed Through Generalization

Beliefs are often the guiding force which tells us what will lead to pain or pleasure. For instance, when something happens to you, the brain asks two questions: "Will this lead to pleasure or pain?" and "what must I do avoid pleasure or pain?" The answer to these questions relies on our beliefs and we form beliefs through generalization. Generalization directs all our actions and determines the direction and quality of our lives. These generalizations help to simplify our lives. For instance, what allows you to drive a car? You sit in the driver's seat and stare at the steering wheel, gear, and ignition, and it becomes familiar to you even when the car model is different. Your experience of driving a car gives you creates a sense of generalization when it comes to driving other cars.

Your Beliefs Have the Power to Build or Destroy

I want you to know something right now: it is never the events of your life, nor is it your environment. However, the meaning and interpretation you attach to the events are what shapes you into who you are. Beliefs are the difference between a hero and a villain; the haves and the have-nots. It's the difference between those that are happy and unhappy. For example, have you ever noticed how people gravitate toward you when you feel happy within yourself? It's almost as if you have a brilliant sun shining within you. Conversely, when you feel gloomy, it's almost as if people shy away from you.

Your beliefs can influence your external environment and bend them to your will. More so, we all can take any experience, beautiful or not, and create a meaning that can either save our lives or destroy it. There are people who have passed through traumatic experiences such as rape or abuse. Instead of letting these bad moments define them, they took the stand to protect those who must pass through the same moments. Some lose their loved ones to devastating illness and created shelters to protect those who are suffering from diseases. That, I believe, is their way of creating lemonade out of the lemon life has so graciously offered to them.

Everyone can tap into those bad situations and channel them into positive endeavors to become better. Sadly, many people never get to tap into it. Many people don't even recognize their bad beliefs. If you don't adopt the faith that there's a reason for all the tragedies in life, then you will never truly live. Always look for the silver lining. I know life doesn't always turn out the way you want due to circumstances beyond your control. But you can determine the lessons you want to learn from these experiences. Some Holocaust victims were able to survive because they chose not to determine their lives by the action of those soldiers.

Even in psychology, beliefs can cause biochemical changes in the body. Several studies in multi-personality disorders show that the potency of belief of these patients' belief they have become a new person, resulted in massive changes in their biochemistry. There are several studies that documents the patient's eyes changing as they assume a new identity. Even diseases, such as high blood pressure and diabetes, appear and disappear in tandem to the person's belief as to which identity they're impersonating.

It is common for some to develop the "life is unfair" mentality. These people develop a limiting set of beliefs about who they are and what they are capable of. Because they've experienced failure multiple times, they believe they won't be able to succeed in the future. More so, they tend to focus on being "realistic" out of fear of failure and pain. People who often say, "life is unfair" or "let's be realistic" are afraid of being hurt again. They also restrain themselves from going all out on a project because they think failure is a constant in their lives. Sadly, it is the same reason why sets of realistic people will rarely get to the top of their niche. Leaders, on the other hand, are rarely realistic. They are intelligent and are not realistic by other people's standards.

The Danger of Looking Through the Social Mirror

The world will always find a way to give you a label. Sadly, most people let themselves be defined by these labels. More so, it becomes so limiting that we accept it as our truth. How many times have you let people decide what you are, what you can do without having a say in it? Once, twice, perhaps all your life? Sadly, most people base their beliefs in life on the current social paradigm, based on people's perception and opinion about them. Here's a question for you: have you ever looked at your reflection through those disjointed mirrors at a carnival? Do you get a perfect reflection of yourself? Hell no!

People would say, "you are crazy," "you will never amount to anything," "you eat like a pig," "why are you so dull?" etc.

Perhaps, you might come across a plethora of such paradigms from people. However, just like disjointed mirrors in a carnival, people's opinions are not a true reflection of whom and what you are. It is often a projection of the character and weakness of people giving the input.

Sometimes, social paradigms claim that we are largely determined by the conditions. Furthermore, these social paradigms postulate that we have no control over the circumstances of our lives. Yes, we all agree that these social paradigms influence our decisions. However, they do not control our lives. To back up these claims, society has created three social maps to explain the nature of man. Sadly, these social maps are accepted globally.

The 3 Social Maps

Genetic determinism is another way of society telling us that some of our circumstances are created by our grandparents. They try to tell you that you inherited your fiery temper from your grandparents. In other words, they say it's in your DNA. It goes from generation to generation.

Psychic determinism, also described as the Freudian psychology, is the social map that says your parents did it to you. Your childhood experience and your upbringing will lay out your tendencies and character structure. They explain everything based on how you were brought up. For example, if you are afraid to speak in front of a crowd or feel self-conscious whenever you do something in front of people, some will say it is because you were castigated and emotionally brutalized when you were a kid. This is a common example of psychic determinism.

Emotional determinism says that your life is a product of your environment and those who surround you. It says your boss, wife, your nation, the economic situation, and circle of friends are the reason for your present condition. Going back to the example of Jake and Mark, we cannot deny that the environment influences their decision. However, Jake was able to rise above the environmental determinism; he was able to transform his environmental paradigm into the fuel for his success. Conversely, Mark was satisfied with the environmental determinism.

Each of these maps is based on the concept that we are conditioned to react in a certain way to a specific stimulus. Failure to break from these limiting beliefs can lead to depression and unhappy life. You must be proactive.

Take the Initiative to Change Your Story: Become Proactive

Enough of the sad story: it is time to stop complaining about your circumstances. Rather, I want you to look at all things you think are unfair in your life. Picture them right now. Now, think of what you desire in your life; a promotion, a better job, a new house, more money, children, and a healthy lifestyle. Since you now have a clear picture of what you desire to change, I want you to imagine squashing those circumstances. Yes, bury them beneath your desire for a better life. This is about you are taking the initiative; to refuse to be defined by your circumstances. Realize that you are the architect of your life and make your dreams happen. Humans by nature are proactive. If your life is a function of your circumstance and condition, it is because you have chosen to empower those factors.

Furthermore, you become reactive to every external stimulus. Reactive people are affected by their physical and social environment. For example, if the weather is bad, they feel bad. However, proactive people carry their own ray of sunshine with them. They don't care if it rains or not; they feel indifferent. What's more? They are value driven.

Reactive people are susceptible to the social environment. As mentioned earlier they are reactive to people's opinion and perceptions about them. If people treat them well, they feel well. When they don't, they become protective or defensive. By depending on people emotionally, reactive people are allowing other people's weaknesses to control them.

Mind you, I'm not saying proactive people are immune to these external impulses. Rather, their response to the stimulus is entirely value-based.

Remember, no condition can control or determine your fate unless you allow it.

So, take the initiative. I'm not saying you should be aggressive, pushy, or obnoxious. It means recognizing your power to effect change. Take our time to study more, take more aptitude tests, read books, have more interest in your work, invest more in your family; these are the proactive tasks I want to you take. More so, I want you to do more. Your condition was never holding you back. Rather, you are the one holding on these circumstances as a crutch to defend your inactions. Want to become better? Be proactive Be responsible. The world is a place filled with fairy tales and reality, but it is never unfair!

Chapter 4:
Embrace the Hurdles in Life

The Boogeyman Is Back!

This time, he is not hiding in our closet or underneath the bed. He is no longer restricted to nighttime or our nightmares; rather, we see him in the light of the day. While growing up, we thought we were finally free of the boogeyman. However, we see it in all its ugliness and monstrosity; we see it when we wake up, on our way to our office. Sometimes we close our eyes to avoid looking at this monstrosity, but we still see it in our mind. Gradually, it wears us down as we ask ourselves, "what does it want with me?" Yet, we never looked it in the eye. We've never even asked about its mission. We prefer to huddle in fear as it blocks our path. Sadly, some might never face the boogeyman all their lives, while others are forced to face it.

The boogeyman in this example is the hurdles and obstacles we face daily. Unlike the boogeyman of our childhood fantasies, this is real, and the realization scares us to the bone. We all know that hurdles come in different forms and magnitude. Some challenges or hurdles might come in the form of financial barriers, where your dreams and aspirations are cut short due to insufficient funds. More so, it could be due to physical disadvantages. Also, it could be due to rising un-employment, a decayed educational experience system, an examination, and even a toxic relationship. Whatever these hurdles are, they all serve one purpose: to block our dreams and goals. Irrespective of your status or station in life, these obstacles are a constant. It is the main constant of human evolution, and it will still be there long after you are gone. When we, however, do face it, we are left with two choices: we either sit in a corner paralyzed by our fears of the obstacle, or we rise to the challenge and face it? So, I'm asking you: which would you rather choose, the former or the latter? Do you want to know your answer? You will choose the latter. Everyone would go for the latter. Why? It's because we all want to achieve our goals and we know the only way to do that is to embrace our hurdles. However, most people tend to dream and fantasize about their goals, without the thought of rising to the challenge. They prefer to watch in awe and celebrate those who rise above the same hurdles they are so scared of. More so, some go down a dark path by blaming their lives, relationships, jobs, environment, parents, and everything that surrounds them for their predicament. As mentioned in the previous chapter, it's time to stop looking at the world as if it's unfair. Rather, it's time to embrace the scary boogeyman. It's time for you to stop seeing it as your enemy

Acknowledge the Obstacles Before You

Do you why we prefer to huddle in fear before our obstacles while fantasizing about a possible solution? It's because we let our obstacles define us and hold us back. Our physical height, weight, age, relationship, and even what people think about us, are some of the obstacles we face. No doubt, we all have faced unique obstacles, but have you taken a moment for those who came before you. History is overflowing with athletes who are considered too small for their niche, pilots with dreadful eyesight, racial disadvantaged people, school dropouts, dyslexics, and dreamers ahead of their time. Perhaps you've also come across stories of those who grew up in a worse environment, where their very existence was being threatened.

Here's a question for you: what happened to them? Well, many gave up along the way. But a few didn't. They practiced harder at overcoming their challenges. Their obstacles honed their skills in looking for weak spots and shortcuts. Yes, they were tossed around to the point where they nearly gave up. Do you know why and how they triumphed? They saw their obstacles as an opportunity. Hold on! They didn't stop at that; they took the step to do something special about it. These set of people give us hope. Their stories help cement the fact that it is impossible to surmount any obstacle. These stories show us they were able to achieve victory via a cocktail of creativity, daring, and focus. Want to know what's more surprising? These people never had access to the plethora of information you have at your disposal. Want to know more? Some were even born with zero chance of success.

Right now, I want to look at those things that stand in your way; look right at it and don't back away. Hold on! Don't blame it. Don't hate it. Rather, embrace it and see it as the passage to your next step. Funny, right? You may say, "I can embrace my disability or disadvantage." Yes, you can. History has proved it to us, and you can do it, too. Are you ready to explore the next phase? Then, let's see the first step you need to take in embracing your hurdles.

Harness the Discipline of Perception

Why do we keep coming back to this word: perception? It's because perception is the one concept that separates the successful from those who are not. It is simply the way you see the world. If you see it as a cold place filled with cheats and crooks, then you will come across those who exhibit that trait. What's more? Even if they aren't, your mind will still interpret according to your perception. John Rockefeller was one of those who saw the world differently: he saw it as a place filled with boundless opportunities. Throughout his lifetime, he never got flustered during chaotic events. Rather, he prospered and soared. He surely wasn't the most brilliant. Rather, he chose to learn from market crashes and depressions. In life, we will surely come across obstacles, but what matters is our reaction to it. And our reaction stems from our perception, which is the way we see the problem. Where one sees a crisis, another sees opportunity. Where some are blinded by the glamor and blitz of success, some see reality with ruthless objectivity. You must realize that every reaction and emotion you experience are functions of your perception.

I know it's not so easy.

Yes, we live in a different time and a gilded age. We have experienced two major economic crashes, exponential rates in unemployment, and a concurrent rise in housing costs. Global warming and erratic weather conditions plague our daily life.

These occurrences have a negative toll on people, and they breed negative emotions. However, the ball is in your court; you can decide to look beyond the outward appearances. Yes, you can learn to cut through the illusion of the problems that seem to overwhelm us. Discipline in perception is what you need to look beyond the illusion. This will help you to see the advantage and the proper course of action to take in the face of an obstacle. With this, you will never be a slave to your fears or impulses. You can achieve this by transforming that disadvantage into a fortune, skill set, or education. Here are a few tips to help you harness the discipline of perception.

Firstly, learn to be objective. Secondly, learn to keep your emotions at a keen level. Thirdly, steady your nerves and ignore what limits others. Furthermore, choose to see the good in all situations and focus on what you can control.

Recognize Your Strength

I want you to know that you are never completely powerless. Even when it seems as if all is lost, we are still in control of our minds. The ball is in our court whether you are going to break or survive. The world can label you, call you handicap, poor or unfit, but it doesn't matter. Popular figures such as Malcolm X, Nelson Mandela, and so many others have come to understand this fundamental distinction. They were able to turn a prison into a workshop where they transformed themselves, and the education center where they could educate others. When you have your wits around, you can step back and realize that there's a silver lining to every situation. For instance, let's say an employee made a drastic mistake that cost you a fortune. I'm sure this is a situation you've spent so much time and effort to avoid. Instead of you being a lament about the loss, change your perspective. See this situation as an opportunity to break beyond the barrier and to rise.

Live in The Present

Do you want to know a secret? Many great corporations like Microsoft, LinkedIn, Hewlett-Packard, Charles Schwab, Walt Disney Company, and so many more, started operation during economic and stock market crashes. Surprising? When others are closing shop, these pioneers were creating companies. Why? Because the founders were busy living in the present. Surely, they didn't know if it will get better or worse, but they just knew what was going to work.

They knew they had a great idea, and they took steps to make it work. However, most people aren't content to deal with things as they happen. They prefer to trouble themselves with what is fair or not, what's behind this or that, and what others are doing. By the time they get worked up over inane things, they have little-to-no energy to deal with their problems. As explained in the previous chapter, most people start with a disadvantage, and they perform well. Why? Because they took things step-by-step.

Focus on the present and not the imaginary boogeyman that might be ahead or not. Rather, take every day one step at a time. It doesn't matter whether you are in a good or bad job market. It doesn't matter if this is the worst time to be alive. What matters is to embrace your obstacle by living in the moment. Moreover, the more you embrace your hurdles, the easier they become.

It's not enough to live in the moment—you must work at it. Discard distracting thoughts and catch your mind when it wanders off. As you do this, I want you to remember that this moment is not your life. Rather, it's just a moment in your life. Ignore why the problem is happening to you and focus on what's in front of you.

Get Moving

"Oh! It's not yet time; I'm still waiting for the right moment." "Perhaps, it's not my turn yet." These are the common excuses you will hear from those around you. Some might say, "I can't launch this business idea until I have a million dollars" or "I can't be happy until I have enough money to buy my dream house or visit my vacation destination." Let me ask you this: what would have happened to the racial discrimination in the States if Civil Rights activists like Martin Luther King Jr. and Rosa Parks said it wasn't time yet? People like Amelia Earhart weren't satisfied with just sitting in the sidelines in a profession dominated by men. Rather, she chose to defy the odds and break the stereotype. She didn't care that the world said it wasn't time for women. Instead, she took the step and became the first woman to fly solo across the transatlantic. This accomplishment wouldn't have occurred if she didn't take that step.

Most times, we know what our problems are. We may even know what to do about them. However, we fear that acting is too risky; that we are not experienced or capable enough.

Let me tell you the truth: the right moment will never come. So, I want you to tell yourself: the time for my excuses is over. The bell is rung, and it is time to start moving.

We often have the misconception that the world moves at our pace. So, we delay when we should initiate action. We tip-toe when we should be running and soaring above the skies. Then, we get surprised when the breakthrough never occurs. It is at this moment when the enemies can get their act together. While you are relaxing and thinking of a thousand reasons why you can't act, someone somewhere is building a plan that would put you out of business. This is not the time to get comfortable and to rest on your oars. Rather, it's the time to keep moving, even when the obstacle won't budge, and even when you get frustrated in the pursuit of your goals. It's time to walk the talk.

See the Education in Your Defeat

If you think that you can always move your obstacles on the first try, you are wrong. Sometimes, it takes repeated efforts and strategies to clear away the problem. This concept is why most startups in Silicon Valley succeeded. These startups don't launch a product with polished and completed features. Instead, they introduce their Minimum Viable Product (MVP), which is the most basic version of their product with minimal features into the market. The purpose of this concept is to gauge their customers' response. If the response is bad, they go back to the drawing board and improve the product based on their customers' feedback. These innovative individuals have changed their perception of obstacles.

They see failure or setback as an opportunity to improve their designs. It's no surprise that these startups are growing at an exponential rate. Therefore, it's time to see yourself as a startup; change the way you view failure. See it as part of your journey toward your destination. Every success story is preceded by scores of failures. These successful people that you read about today aren't ashamed of their failures. Rather, they saw the education in it and devised new ways to conquer it—it's that simple.

Yes, I know failure hurts. However, I'm sure we can all admit that temporary and anticipated failure hurts less than permanent or catastrophic failure. When you expect failure along your path, you will be better prepared to handle it when it occurs. When it comes, be glad to pay the cost and have the hope that this is not the end of your journey. However, if you fail to learn from your failures, you will watch as your dreams sift through your fingers like sand.

Take A Walk

Want to know a final secret to embrace your hurdles? Take a walk, exercise more, or do something that will take your mind off the magnitude of the challenge. Richard Branson, when asked about the secret to his productivity, said he exercises daily. It is vital to find a way to clear your head either via a walk or through exercises. More so, you can practice meditation to ease the stress of your daily routine; in fact, so many studies allude to the soothing benefits of exercising on the brain. Exercises fill you with a sense of euphoria—also commonly known as endorphins—which enables you to take on other tasks. More so, it helps gives you a clear perspective on the obstacle you are so scared of.

Chapter 5:
Uncomfortable Means Opportunity

Your hands are shaking as you hold the speech in your hands. It is almost time for you to climb up the lectern, and it feels as if you might pass out at any moment. Sweat droplets bead across your eyebrows and streak down your back. Even your armpits are not left out from this "waterfall." You tell yourself over and over that you can do it. Since you've practiced a lot before a mirror, this should be easy. Then, another thought crosses your mind, and you curse the day you accepted the task. Alas, it's your company's dinner party, and you've been chosen to represent your team to deliver a speech. From your position at the back of the hall, you can see the company's executives and other important dignitaries. Even your family members are around to cheer on. Oh no! The compere just called your name. As you walk toward the stage, it's as if your legs are filled with lead: every step is heavy and unbearable. You ask yourself, "How am I walking properly? What are they saying about me? Was that chuckle meant for me?" Before you know it, you are already on the stage. "Everyone is watching," you tell yourself in trepidation. At that moment, every quip you've lined up to break the ice is practically out the window.

However, you decide to soldier on and deliver the speech as best you can. It was a shock when you were greeted by a standing ovation at the end of your speech. All through the dinner event, people couldn't stop talking about how brilliant you were on the stage. The executives keep stealing glances at you, while your team members are showering you with praise. However, you are still in a daze. As the euphoria of the experience wears off, you remember how scared you were before the speech. You remember how you decided to take on the task when others shied away from it. You've never done anything like that before.

You return to the office the next day, and your boss couldn't stop thanking you for making the team proud. Later that month, you have successfully represented the company in different capacities. Now, you have a new office to yourself with greater responsibility and higher pay. Then, you ask yourself one more time, "How did I get here?"

Yes, how did this individual move from grass to grace; from the back of the queue to the front. Well, it's simply because he sacrificed his comfort to break forth from his daily routine. He decided to step out of his normal routine; and at that moment, he cemented his fate. By leaving his comfort zone, he was able to accomplish what would take years in just a month. Most times, we fail to realize the abundance of potential within us because we fear the unknown. Without even trying, we just prefer to keep on living without a taste for more. And this is how we become stagnant.

Opportunities Lie Beyond Your Comfort Zone

Life is a great teacher, overflowing with so many opportunities waiting for us to grab them and to own them. However, most of us never see these opportunities. We deny their existence and claim that opportunities are just like kid's stories. So, why do we deny the existence of opportunities? Why is it so much easier to blame the system and everything wrong in it? Why do we fail to notice that those who have made their mark on history have passed through the same circumstance? More so, do you realize that most successful people have had it worse than you?

Yes, these are the questions that we need to answer. The main reason many fails to rise above their station in life is they are afraid to step outside their comfort zone, which is where opportunities reside. Technology has made everything so much easier. Today, people rarely walk to their destinations as there are a variety of means to make or easier for them. With just a click on an app, you can get an Uber ride to anywhere you want. There's no more hunting or foraging through the wild for food since we can get everything from our nearby mall. Most technology innovations are driven by a need to increase comfort levels. For instance, elevators take away the stress of climbing stairs. Hold on! I'm not complaining about the dishwasher or microwave—I'm not crazy. Yes, it's a natural human instinct to always seek pleasure and to avoid pain and discomfort. Most times, we succumb to these instincts and end up stunting our growth. We must understand that great things happen when we try to take a risk by delving into the unknown. Great things become sweeter when we go through discomfort to achieve them—it's that simple. We wouldn't value opportunities without the pain we passed through before we could attain them. For instance, you can't become a great speaker if you don't take the step to break out of your comfort zone. It's the reason why great speakers like Anthony Robbins are at the top of their niche. In his book, "Awakening the Giant Within," he talks about how he left his comfort zone by reading over 700 books in school. What's more? To become fluent and better at public speaking, he broke the barriers of his comfort zone by taking every speaking job he could get his hands. Within the space of a decade, this former janitor became one of the most celebrated speakers in the world today. What did he do? He stepped out of his comfort zone by embracing discomfort until he achieved his goal.

Comfort Is Overrated!

Every day, we endure the boring routine of our daily activities; we prefer to sit at that job we hate. Yes, we contend ourselves with the race of life in a bid to be comfortable. We forget that man was never meant to be comfortable always. Comfort was only meant for rejuvenation and nothing more. Comfort causes people to close their eyes for one second and find out that they've wasted 30 years. Comfort is what makes the overpaid CEO rest on his achievements, while someone is building the next product to put out of business. Yes, comfort, contentment—whatever you prefer to call it—is overrated. More so, people mistakenly associate it with happiness. We forget that happiness lies in the completion of a daunting task in our discomfort zone. If you asked the person in the illustration above, he would surely tell you he felt happy at the end of the speech. The promotion you've been waiting for lies at the end of that professional course you dread so much. Remember there's nothing wrong with a little discomfort. It's the necessary spice of life to reach your target.

When to Embrace Discomfort

Not every discomfort is worth embracing. You should know that there are different types of discomfort and there are certain situations where these discomforts are classified as helpful and not harmful. To understand this better, here's how to know if the discomfort is the right move for you.

1. Embrace Discomfort When It Feels Safe

Yes, you need to embrace discomfort to tap into potential opportunities. However, you need to practice caution. For instance, a first-time juggler shouldn't start with chainsaws or any other heavy machinery. I understand I'm trying to take you out of your comfort zone. However, it's not an excuse to be foolish. This section is important if you want to encourage yourself to keep stepping out of your comfort zone. It is more difficult to step out of your comfort zone if you immediately get hurt on your first try. This is the time when you must start small and incorporate the small habits, we talked about in the first chapter. You can't start exercising by running a thousand miles the first time. Rather, you start with a mile then you pick up the pace until you can finally reach your goal. Mind you, sometimes life unexpectedly throws us in extremely difficult zones. In this instance, you must ride through it without receding into your shell.

2. Embrace Discomfort When It's Repeatable

In other words, embrace discomfort when you can form a positive habit from it. Discomfort is useful when the situation can be repeated, and these subsequent repetitions will make it more comfortable for you. For instance, starting a new diet like Paleo or Keto is usually hard. To some, this is way into their discomfort zone. You will probably feel like dying in the first two weeks, especially when your body undergoes ketosis—a metabolic state where the body runs on fat instead of sugar. However, this new eating habit will gradually become easy for you to follow. However, if you scald your skin, you might learn a valuable lesson from it and become tougher from the experience, but you wouldn't want to experience it all the time. Why? Because the overall potential for growth via that incident is weak.

There's a clause to this: one-time ventures in discomfort zones can help change your perspective. Perhaps, it can give the "Aha" moment. For instance, some people say a single skydiving experience changed their perspective. Skydiving falls into the discomfort zone, and it's an opportunity to face your fears head-on. It will give you the courage to tackle other areas you fear.

3. Embrace Discomfort When There's A Clear Benefit

Public speaking is uncomfortable, but it boosts your confidence levels. Exercise and a good diet are uncomfortable, but they increase your overall health and fitness. Generally, the benefits of discomfort make you stronger either emotionally, physically, or mentally. So, if you strategically and intentionally expose yourself to difficulty, your body will become accustomed to it as you progress. Mind you, I'm not trying to glorify hardship. We have all experienced one or two things that we wouldn't want to experience again. However, this is to show you the type of discomfort you can introduce into your life.

Still find it difficult to embrace the uncomfortable. Then, you need to incorporate these habits into your daily schedule.

Deep Breathing

Have you ever had a panic attack where you feel as if the walls are closing in on you? The reason why you are hyperventilating is that you were exposed to a stressful situation. Although some of us might not suffer from a panic attack, we lose focus during these situations. Well, not to worry. According to recent studies, taking slow deep breaths can help keep you calm and collected. More so, it distracts you from the uncomfortable situation and helps you to feel at peace. Here's how to do the deep breathing exercise: inhale and count to 5, then slowly exhale for about 7 seconds. How do you feel now? At that moment of completing the breathing exercise, the uncomfortable situation becomes less threatening to you.

A Few Seconds of Distraction Will Change the Scales

Most people see distraction as one of the obstacles to achieving their goals. Well, they are right. Too much of a distraction can derail you from your target. However, just a little dose of distraction is needed before you decide, especially when you feel uncomfortable. It's common practice for people to take a break in an office meeting, especially when people are becoming more uncomfortable. You can replicate this action by using a few minutes to help you gather your thoughts. You can focus on something you love to take your mind off the uncomfortable situation. This is the same principle doctors use when giving immunization shots to kids: they distract them from the task at hand by offering them a toy.

Be Kind to Yourself

I can't emphasize this enough. The world is already unfair as it is, you don't want to add to the baggage. No one is going to love you or understand you as much as you do. When faced with an uncomfortable situation, it's alright to feel scared. But don't ever criticize yourself. Here's a trick I use during this situation: I would imagine what I'd tell someone else passing through the same situation. I'll write it down and read it to myself—trust me, it works! Remember, be kind to yourself and find a way to use your emotions to fuel your actions toward opportunities.

Chapter 6:
Easy Offers No Reward

I am of the school of thought that there are no coincidences in life. I believe that absolutely everything that happens in life happens for a reason. This, therefore, makes it important that you grab opportunities each time you come across them. While some opportunities come well packaged and are very undeniable, some do not look like what you need. However, they start looking real and important when you begin to unravel them. Now, the truth remains that certain things that are considered opportunities might turn out very differently when unraveled. That notwithstanding, if you give it a try, you will almost have no regret. However, if you fail to check out an opportunity, even if you fail to admit it, you will always be full of regrets concerning how things would have turned out if only you took advantage of an opportunity. You never can tell. Sometimes, throwing caution to the wind is what you need to alter your future positively. While it is always advised that you learn to walk before you run or even fly, you should not take baby steps for too long. There are times when you should take leaps. Now, I am not saying you will always find it easy when you leap. There are, however, times when you must go all out to ensure that your status changes.

When there is life, they say there is hope. Well, if you fail to take risks, you might never get past the stage of hope. While you are alive, you can always take risks. They might not turn out as planned—that's what makes them risks in the first place.

Sometimes, taking it easy is considered a sign of intelligence. As much as this is arguable, taking it easy is also a sign of fear and the absence of courage. If you think you have a lot of fears, now is the time to know that you are not the only one with fears. Everyone has fears. However, what differentiates those that face their fears and those that don't is the ability to take risks.

In the history of the world, there at quite a few people that refuse to take the easy way out. These set of people gave up instant gratification for a long-lasting solution. One of such people is Nelson Mandela.

Nelson Mandela spent 27 years of his time on Earth in prison. He was a freedom fighter that openly opposed apartheid in South Africa. Although he was given the opportunity to walk out of prison and stop any form of demonstration, he chose to remain in prison. Today, the entire black community of South Africa is free from Apartheid because of the actions of Nelson Mandela.

Why Taking Risks Comes with Great Rewards

Dreams are amazing. However, they are not known to come on a platter of gold. If you are very much interested in achieving your dreams—and at the right time, too—there are certain things that you must do. One of the most important is taking risks. It is not just enough to take risks. These risks should be properly calculated and should be worth every step. Regardless of how important it is to take chances and go through risks in life, there are lots of people that are still very scared of taking the first step.

The reward for risk might be promising. Nevertheless, it is called a risk because there is a huge likelihood that you will part with something if your plan does not fall through. When risks are involved, anything can be lost. In a business setting, when you take a risk, the most likely thing to be lost if your plans do not follow through is money. However, beyond the loss of money, there are other things of value that can be lost. Popular among them is your reputation and your time. Well, amazingly, these very things (time, reputation, and money) are some of the things that you will gain when you take calculated risks. The many gains that are associated with calculated risks can completely transform your life and business.

There are countless benefits associated with taking risks. Some are indeed obvious and stare us in the face; while others are quite hidden and must be discovered.

When you make taking calculated risks a part of your routine, in no time you will become open to both opportunities and challenges. When done regularly, the barriers in your mind soon wear away, and you discover that you now have new mental limits along with a much-improved mental capacity.

Not many people know one way to build creativity is by taking risks. When you place yourself on the spot, your creative juices tend to flow much better than you can even imagine. This takes place because, in the absence of any excuses, it gets easy to try out something new.

It is a good thing to have a big picture of what you want. There is no rule against seeing the end of your plan right from the beginning of it. Nonetheless, not everything can be perfectly planned. You should leave some space for spontaneity. Spontaneity does not just offer you a well-deserved result when it works out; it also helps you have some fun while going through a major challenge. It is crucial to note that the chance of pulling something off when trying it for the first time is not always one hundred percent. Nonetheless, the chances are higher when you give it nothing but your best shot.

Despite what many people think, risks are not taken in the absence of logic. That is why they are better described as calculated risks. In the face of risks, it becomes much easier to come up with a definition of what it is that you want. Risks are not just taken; they are accompanied by some serious considerations. Also, taking a risk makes you want to ensure that things work out. In the absence of risks, individuals might not be sure if what they are going for is exactly what they want. However, in the presence of risks, there is always some sort of assurance that what you are going for is something that you really want.

One thing that taking risks does for you helps you break free from mediocrity and the attitude of playing safe. Risk takers never try to stay safe. They are known for forging ahead continuously in business and their chosen career paths. Risks do not just help you accomplish things; they also go a long way in building your confidence.

One thing is noteworthy: there are no guarantees in life. Sometimes, all you must do is trust your instincts and take that risk. It might not pan out well; however, you can try out the same thing several times and finally get a result.

How to Engage in Risks

Life is about taking risks. Everyone has taken risks at some point in their lives. The first risk most people take is learning to walk as a baby. When a baby learns to walk, there is no guarantee that the baby will not fall. Regardless, the baby still attempts walking. Children, in general, are not new to the idea of taking risks. Well, surprisingly, this ability to take risks reduces with age. The fact that babies must engage in risks before they can make their first step means humans were designed to take risks. Now a question arises: how can one engage in risks?

There are numerous ways to take risks. Regardless of the type of risk taken, one thing must be done first: you must evaluate the risks. Evaluating a risk properly is the only way to take a calculated risk. A lot of people fear taking risks because when risks are taken, it means they are not fully in charge of what the outcome of a situation will be. Now, taking risks does not necessarily mean going all out to get something done without first giving it thought. It simply means thinking something through intelligently and deciding that it is worth trying out. With the right amount of confidence in your abilities, taking risks and recovering from risks can be done easily.

To take a calculated risk, put down all the possible outcomes that can result from taking that risk. This should include positive outcomes, as well as negative outcomes. While at this, always bear in mind that a lot of the possibilities are associated with the risk you are about to take will not see the light of day. You should try to come up with a solution in case any of the negative possibilities that are associated with the risk you are about to take.

When trying to decide between two options (i.e., choosing between two jobs), you can't see the future. To take a calculated risk and make the right choice, consider the pros and cons of the two jobs. Once done, you should pick the job which has more pros than cons. As much as there is no guarantee that you made the right choice, the job with more pros is most likely the better one for you. This does not necessarily mean it will be right for someone else.

If you are unable to overcome the fear of disappointment, you will never be able to take a risk. The fear of disappointment can be said to be an ingredient for a life full of regrets.

If you work in a department in a firm and are not comfortable with the department you work in, you can ask for a change. Now, if you ask for a change, you cannot tell what response you will get. You might get a "yes"; or you might also get a "no." Well, if you get a "yes," that will be nice. However, if you get a "no," it will be a disappointment. That, however, will not change who you are. With a "no", you might even get an idea of how well you have been performing on your job.

Risks are never comfortable. When you are out of your comfort zone, you become more comfortable when faced with an uncertain situation. Now, the inability to tell what the outcome of an event will be can make one anxious. Regardless of this, the longer you are out of your comfort zone, the less anxious you will be in the middle of uncertainty.

A simple way of starting with this is to write down a list of uncertainties in your life. Ensure you write them down from the most anxious to the least anxious. Now, when you have them written down, begin to face these situations on purpose from the least uncertain to the most uncertain.

Basic Facts You Need to Know About Taking Risks

The path of which is associated with risks is a path that a lot of people fear taking. The reason for this is it is a path that not many people have gone through. This means it does not have a clearly defined track for people to walk through. The implication of this is the easiest way to get through this part successfully is to rely on your instincts. Unfortunately, our instincts are not always right and can make us do the wrong things sometimes. Amazingly, the opportunities which are usually on roads that have not been traveled by many people are usually untapped. As a result of this, the few people that are ready to take the risk to go through this path are usually highly rewarded.

Often, the disappointments we face when we take risks do not have much to do with us. If they have anything to do with us at all, it is usually just a little. Most disappointments we experience when we take risks are associated with other factors aside from us. As a result of this, when we take calculated risks, there is little to nothing we can do to alter the outcome. Not taking a risk is as good as being disappointed because of a risk taken. The reason for this is with risks, disappointments are usually instantaneous. However, in the absence of risks, disappointments still occur. This time, they occur after a long time and might not give you any chance to recover.

In as much as the best way to get the best out of a situation is to be always prepared for such a situation. There are times when we must make moves even if we are not prepared. Although preparing ahead of time is believed will help anyone get the best out of a situation, this is not always the case. In some situations, disappointments still occur even after adequate preparations. In this same way, one can get the best out of a situation by just following their instincts and not having any real form of preparation.

Risks will not always turn out positive. When we take risks and succeed, it is a good thing. However, when we take risks and fail, we only fail when we give up. If we don't give up, we will figure out a different way to get things to work; it will just take a little more time.

When you take a risk, there is no guarantee that things will pan out as planned. This is more reason you should take risks earlier in life. If you take a risk early and things go south, you will always have time to get back on your feet. However, if you take a risk quite late, you really might never get back on your feet if things go bad.

Chapter 7:
Judging A Book by Its Cover Will Be Your Downfall

The average person knows that judging others is not exactly a good thing. Why do I know this? Well, nobody wants to be judged; everyone wants to be understood. To a large extent, we are all guilty of judging others. While at this, however, only very few of us realize that judging others can lead to our downfall.

Imagine you come across a seemingly harmless beggar on the street, and you think such a person is too healthy to be begging anyway. You get close to this beggar, and they take out a gun and point at you. You are surprised and must flee. Well, a few days later, the news gets to you that the beggars around the place you met a beggar are usually victims of kidnappers. Suddenly, your perception of this beggar will change. You formerly judged them for begging because you thought they could do better. You were even more surprised when the beggar pulled a gun. Well, with the knowledge that beggars are usually victims of kidnappers, you understand the situation better, and it all makes perfect sense to you. This is not a real-life situation. It does, however, gives you an idea of what judging people is like.

You see, ideally when you come across someone that you feel is too good to be begging, instead of being judgmental, you should have questions on your mind. These questions can be "why are they begging? What can you do to help?" In as much as being judgmental is more of an instinct than asking questions regarding why people are in certain situations, it is important to train yourself to exhaust all alternatives before speaking.

So, with a mindset that is more compassionate and less judgmental, when you see someone that you consider too good to be begging, you can see the situation differently. As soon as you see this individual, you are curious and do not judge. You begin to wonder why they are begging in the first place and what can be done to help them. Now, even if you fail in helping them, you will not give them a proud look.

As a person, it is expedient that you learn to look beyond people's backgrounds and their present states. Seeing the potential in people is good quality. Give people opportunities instead of judging them.

Why Do People Judge Others?

Although a lot of us might not admit this fact, somewhere in our subconscious, we think that individuals with the same physical appearance have the same type of behavior. This is perhaps why it is easy to hate an individual that looks like someone that hurt you in the past.

Now, people associating certain behavior to a certain physical appearance might be common when looks are involved. Nonetheless, it does not end at that. Peoples speech pattern, their way of walking, and even the way they dress can make it easy to associate them with a certain type of behavior. If while growing up, someone that was repeatedly nice to you was known for wearing a shape of prescriptive lenses, there is a tendency that you will be very comfortable with people that wear that shape of prescriptive lenses. This is irrespective of what you have heard about them.

When you come across a person, the first thing you probably notice is such a person's body language and physical appearance. Irrespective of the fact that that is not all we see; a lot of people do not realize this.

As individuals, sometimes we forget some things. However, when we come across people that remind us of some of these experiences, the memories come rushing back. If you had a negative experience with someone and you meet another person that has some striking similarities with the person that hurt you, it is just natural that you will dislike this new person. Now, if this person does something that is slightly hurtful, you are most likely going to overreact because you will be associating their action with that of someone that you already dislike.

In as much as the reason above, if one of the generally accepted reasons why people judge others, it is not the only reason. Sometimes, we judge people because they have certain characteristics which we really will never accept from ourselves. A simple example is this: When a shy person meets an outgoing person, even if that outgoing person is not a show-off, it is almost natural for the shy person to judge them as being too loud. Generally, shy people will never be the center of attention. As a result of this, when another person is always the center of attention, they might consider that person a show-off.

Judging Others Is Bad for You

Not everyone knows this, but judging other people is bad for them. It ruins their reputation without even giving them a chance to prove themselves. Well, judging others is not only bad for them, but it is also bad for you. You might not realize this, but there are lots of negative effects of judging others on the individual carrying out judgment.

It is amazing how there are good judgments and bad judgments. Still, most people dwell on just bad judgments. Often, bad judgments are carried out on people's physical appearances, religion, social status, skin color, and dressing.

Always judging others is a habit; just like other bad habits, it can be stopped. When you judge others, you are doing yourself so much harm. You know why? You are stopping your mind from seeing both sides of a person. When done constantly, it makes you myopic, and you end up having a closed mind. Now, being close-minded is almost as bad as being uneducated.

If you judge others before getting to know them, you should know one thing for sure: the problem is not with them, the problem is with you.

A lot of people are of the idea that judging others ends with just strangers or people that you do not know well. Well, contrary to that thought, when judging others becomes a habit for you, it is only a matter of time before you start judging individuals that are very close to you. This soon degenerates to a lack of appreciations and ultimately dissatisfaction. When you become judgmental of the people around you, it will put a strain on your relationships.

Now, if you have a strained relationship with people that are closest to you, no one will view you in a positive light. According to research, the ability of an individual to always see the best in other people says a lot about such a person's personality. Seeing the positive side of people is associated with being kind-hearted, emotionally stable, and happy. The exact opposite can be said about people that are always in the habit of judging others, especially when this judgment is negative.

When you see the positive side of other people, it is proof that you have lots of positive traits. However, when all you see is the negative side of people, you can be certain that a lot of people have negative views about you.

When you constantly judge people in front of other people, it is only normal for your audience to assume that you will judge them in front of others, too. The reason for this is quite straight forward: a lot of people will feel that if you can talk poorly to them about other people, then you can say bad things to others about them. This will make them distrust you.

People Are Not Who You Think They Are

Have you heard the saying, "don't judge a book by its cover?" Appearances are often misleading and are not always an accurate representation of who people are. Going by this, you should never judge people by their appearance. Some appear the way they do because they want to always maintain a low key. Others, because they cannot afford expensive things. Regardless of how peoples' appearances are, always consider the good they have done before concluding them.

Reasons Why You Should Not Judge Other People

There are lots of reasons—possible inexhaustible—why judging other people is bad. Most people judge individuals that they know little-to-nothing about. You see, it is important that you know people quite well before ever attempting to judge them. It is rather unfortunate that most people do the exact opposite of that.

People differ in many ways. Even siblings that have been raised in the same house differ in very striking ways. If by chance, you do not enjoy taking part in an activity, it does not necessarily mean that other people do not love that activity. Take this as an example. If you do not like to braid your hair as a guy, it does not mean other people have to hate the same thing. It is wrong for you to go on and tell people that their braided hair does not look great. If you have a university degree and some other person does not, it does not imply that they could not pass their examinations, or they do not know the value of education. It could simply mean that they could not afford to pay for a university education. You see, we differ in lots of ways. The fact that people are different from you does not mean that you are right, and they are wrong.

There are certain people that are indeed better than those around them—this fact notwithstanding, no one that is perfect. There are, however, people that believe that they are perfect. As a result of this, they go on to judge everyone around them and have a habit of always picking on other people's mistakes. Before going ahead to criticize anyone's actions, you should be certain that this criticism is constructive and not merely to bring such person down.

Judging others may come with a feeling of guilt. There are just a handful of people that do not feel guilty when they judge others. Those people are usually regarded as horrible, and I want to assume that they are not a horrible person. I am assuming they are not a horrible person because you are going through this write-up.

Now that you recognize guilt associated with judging others, it is important that you get the best out of this feeling. There is a tendency to let this feeling overwhelm you; however, what you need to do is make it a weapon to serve as an impediment to the attitude of judging others.

Searching for A Reason to Stop Judging People, Well, Here's One

If you have made judging people a habit, one of the best things you can do is to stop judging people. Well, it is one thing to want to quit judging people and another thing to know exactly how to stop judging people.

The first step for anyone that wants to stop judging people is to be aware they're judging. If you are unaware of a bad habit, how are you going to stop?

Picture this: You have a distant relative that has just gone through a very painful breakup. She is depressed and begins overeating. She does not stop at overeating; she also begins drinking. She does all this to mask the pain of the breakup. Her health starts failing, yet she does not stop the bad habits of drinking and overeating. At this point, you may judge her for the bad habits she has. You think she is responsible for her bad health.

Now, the truth remains that her habits are wrong and will not cause a change of any form. Regardless, she does not deserve to be judged. There is a huge likelihood of your awareness of the bad things she is doing to herself. However, you might be ignorant of the root cause of those habits. Well, what is taking place is your relative has just gone through a breakup and is now depressed. She tries to eat and drink to make herself feel happy and take away the pain. We all do things to make ourselves happy when we go through difficulties, even if these things are not so bad for our health.

It takes a lot of practice for you to stop judging people. It is a very bad thing to judge. Sometimes you do not have to tell others about the negative attitude of some people before you judge them. If you find yourself constantly complaining about an individual, then you are most likely judging such an individual.

Once you discover that you are judging someone, there are questions that you must ask yourself, including: "What are the reasons I am judging?" Do I have expectations that are unrealistic?" Do I know what the person am judging is going through?" What do I love about the person I am judging?" How would I act if I were in the shoes of the person I am judging?"

As soon as you are done asking yourself all these questions, ask yourself how you can be of aid to the person. Does this person have any needs? Most times, the person you are judging has some real needs. Other times, all they need is someone that will listen to them and accept them for who they are.

You see, if you must be of help to the people you judge, you can't go on judging them. You cannot only come to their aid when you keep judging them but see what they go through with eyes of empathy. The amazing part of this is that as soon as you are curious about what they are going through and are successfully able to help them, you will be a lot more fulfilled than you will ever be when judging others.

Benefits of Not Judging

When you avoid judging people, you are better focused on your goals. You see, when you put in so much effort and a lot of energy into judging others, you have less time to focus on the things that are important to you. Passing judgment on people makes you think about irrelevant things. You end up spending time on things that are not your business. These things, therefore, take the place of the thoughts you really should be having.

You achieve more when you spend less time judging the world—it's that simple. I'm sure you might say, "I'm not judgmental." Well, here is a question to munch on: have you ever made assumptions about strangers walking down the street? Yes? Such thoughts can separate you from achieving success.

It is quite normal for people to avoid environments where they believe they will be judged. This is not exactly a bad thing. However, if you tend to always judge others, this becomes a major issue. The reason for this is you will always think people will judge you and will do everything to avoid places where you will be judged. This might work for a short while. It will, however, bring about a lot of limitations. The amazing thing is some of the best leaders in the world have been constantly judged. Now, if you avoid certain environments because you think you will be judged, you will be limited by yourself greatly.

Don't ever judge a person by their background. You never really know someone or how much drive they must want to succeed. Always treat them with respect as it could open new opportunities. Measuring a person by their heart and hard work will always preserve.

Chapter 8:
You Can't Conquer the World Alone

Life is a mystery, and the decisions we make either make or mark our lifestyle. The truth is, we are different, and we have various perspectives to solving personal problems. There are no laid down rules in handling personal issues. At some point in our lives, we need a support system to face life challenges squarely—because no one can conquer the world alone.

Certain individuals become emotionally drained when hit to the rocks, while others take it as a steppingstone to run life's race. Just to be clear, we all have our strong and weak moments in life. Additionally, we are designed differently in terms of psychological behavior. But many people are feeble-minded and often are trampled by others. This in a way brings an unconscious lock up because they fear what would become of them when they speak about their phobias and secrets. But you know the truth? It is safer talking to someone about a challenge, especially when it is of a great burden. Also, when the mess is so deep, we need a hand to pull us out from it. Managing emotional stress, breakups, health issues, and depression can be mind-tricky often. We all at some time have fallen victim of this situation. We have unconsciously shut ourselves out from the rest of the world when it was too much to bear.

I, for one, do not dispute the fact that there are situations that warrant personal decisions or lone thoughts. Also, you would agree with me that there are emotional predicaments which require external help from relatives and friends. So, we need to strike a balance to make sure none outweighs the other. When life challenges pop up, building unseen walls or shutting others out should be the least imagination to envisage; this would only be harmful to you. And for this reason, making the right connection in terms of friendships and relationships would be a call of victory to one's emotional and mental metamorphosis.

Choosing the Right Friends

Although some individuals are naturally introverted because they focus primarily on their feelings, it is no reason to have restricted association with others. Studies have shown that humans have a ground-laying need to be associated with others, and "association" can be referred to as "friendship." Just as food is a necessity for human survival, so is friendship.

We perform best when our hunger is quenched, and this is a natural-born instinct because we are social animals. When our social chords are cut off, we become emotionally and physically traumatized. Being without friends poses a danger known as depression. And this intellectual consciousness replays through our brain, leading to an emotional breakdown. Therefore, to face the varied challenges of life, we need to stay motivated with friends.

What is Friendship?

Friendship may be described as a type of relationship distinguished by a feeling of care, affection, and concern between two people. Interestingly, it would surprise you that some friends, in the long run, turn into families. They support us in our down times and put a smile on our face. So, choosing a friend is not something you do hurriedly; it is brain tasking, and of course, it takes time and wisdom to build such a relationship. Although, there are moments when you meet a person, and it feels like you've known them a lifetime; this should not in any way be misinterpreted because not everyone is worth being friends with. Even times when friends become lovers, their attitude changes; a certain number of individuals feel more comfortable with the transition, while others regret the transition. So, maximum caution needs to be taken while choosing the right friend to lean on. An example would be portrayed again in this chapter for a better understanding.

More Than Just Friends

Kimberly and Josh started off as friend's freshman year, and as time passed, the chemistry between them surfaced and grew. They became best friends after a while and had a relationship one would refer to as perfect; of a truth, it was. They were so in love and wanted the whole world to know about it. They connected and understood each other in ways another other couples' thought was impossible. Most of the time, they were seen hanging out together even though they majored in different courses; it was a moment of true friendship for them, and they enjoyed every bit of it. But as semesters swiftly passed, things changed. Everyone thought the two best friends were inseparable. However, they were on the brink of losing their trust and respect for each other. Josh, on his own end, became emotionally attached to someone else while Kimberly thought of ways to salvage the lost hope in their relationship. Oops! Life happens, and it was no one's fault; after all, emotions cannot be totally controlled since it's a raging force on its own.

The sudden change in Josh's new affection shattered her heart, and she became emotionally miserable. He became demanding, selfish, and used every opportunity to demean her before their colleagues and friends. No doubt, he became toxic and suffocating to her. Bit by bit, Kimberly lost her self-confidence until she was engulfed with insecurity and consequently depression.

Alas, she had made Josh her emotional anchor, and now she feels adrift. She literally cried herself to sleep every night and without thorough thought, decided to also be in a new relationship. However, she sought a relationship in her moment of weakness. Yes, she found the wrong set of people, who made her sink deeper into her shell.

Gradually, she found herself abusing drugs and before she knew it, she became addicted.

You can imagine the additional heartache and devastation. The only crime she ever committed was to find love again, but instead, life welcomed her into her cold embrace of filth and disgust. For a long while, the feeling and experience could not be erased from her mind because of the toxicity it had implanted in her. And this, I would say, made her a shadow of herself. She inherently crawled up into a shell and shut the rest of the world out.

So, I would like to ask you, what do you think changed in their relationship?

I'm very certain if Kimberly was given a plain sheet to start all over, she would erase ever meeting Josh. But unluckily, this has become a story she would tell all through her lifetime. Most times, we have no control over emotions, our future, or the people we meet. But most, we have a choice to accept or decline what we want in our lives.

Some relationships have a way of jeopardizing our friendship and can be termed toxic because it affects our mental health. A toxic relationship can be described as a time bomb; it continuously ticks until it someday explodes. It never gets better no matter the effort you put in. Need I say more? A killjoy is what it is. One of the many things it does is confiscate your peace of mind daily. So, I ask, why be in a toxic relationship when you can achieve much more?

Well, we might not make the right choices at the first instance; since everyone puts on their best behavior mode. We are mostly blinded by our emotions and then become victims of the negative outcome of relationships. You have a right to decide what you'd make out of a messed-up life. Different individual's pass-through similar or worse situations than this every day. But the top-notch secrets that have kept them moving with the train of life is their ability to persevere and their capacity to pick up the broken pieces of whatever life was shattered.

Dangers of Loneliness

In line with many experts, loneliness and "being alone" have been interchangeably used to mean the same; but there is a clear distinction between the two words. Loneliness can be a result of several things, but that is not the case with "being alone." For some persons, having a self-timer or being alone can be a choice. As a matter of fact, during my teen years, there were moments I stayed alone. It was not depression or suicidal thoughts taking hold on me; I wanted to be "alone."

Some research has shown that loneliness and unhealthy relationships substantially damage the physical and emotional well-being of a person. And, if not detected and dealt with in time, can pose a great risk to their immune system and mental health. Also, it can lead to several medical complications such as depression, anxiety, and high-level stress; actually, it is a silent health killer. Anyways, it is of great essence to know that no one consciously chooses to be in this state of mind; it gradually creeps in because it is a feeling on its own. More so, because we have no control over it, it gradually turns us into its puppet. Also, death is another factor that contributes to loneliness. This sad feeling can cause psychological trauma for some individuals; especially when the person happens to be a spouse to the deceased. We have various ways of grieving, yes, but others grief more and so suffers setbacks like loneliness.

Deciding

Often, we tend to live in a secluded box we create. And this, I would say, is the greatest harm anyone can cause to themselves emotionally. The choice to speak, to make new friends, to leave for a new location, to try a different relationship, or even a skill can be the best decision to make in a lifetime. Decision making comes along with sacrifices, and surprisingly, not everyone can make sacrifices. So, the big question is: are you ready to make any sacrifice for your happiness? They say talk is cheap, but actions speak louder than voice. Most, there are a quite number of things that need to be taken off the shelf while making life decisions. Also, there are a lot of other things that we need to embrace while coming out of a shell. As unbelievable as they may sound, they have been proven to help individuals overcome toxic relationships and loneliness:

The Gradual Breakthrough

As much as we want to be left with our thoughts, we also need to learn to "let go" of our toxic past. I mean past that would hinder our emotional breakthrough. Do you see it? There are no perfect lives or relationships anywhere. Happy endings only exist in movies and novels. They are nothing but fiction; they never happen in the actual world. In the real world, everyone battles with one hidden character or the other, and it's been since time's past. If you also care to know, we have no Prince Charming or Miss Snow White in this real world. We are all the same evolving individuals trying to salvage our lifestyle to a certain acceptable percentage.

Have A Mentor

Before going into details about what mentorship is, it is necessary to know that not all persons have mentors; this decision does not in any way make them unserious with life pursuit, nor does it mean failure for them; they just do not see it as a necessity or a trophy to be won. These individuals perform better without mentors. In contrary, persons suffering from loneliness or emotional trauma need a lot of mentoring to gradually rehabilitate. What then is mentorship? Mentorship is a type of relationship in which a more knowledgeable person in a carved niche helps a less experienced person. For instance, if I am going through a phase and at the same time feeling depressed, getting a mentor or a person to lean on would help revive my lost hope.

Finally, asking for the big help!

It is one thing to be around friends, mentors, and relatives. Also, it is a different ball game to be able to confide in them. Emotional help does not come cheap; actually, it takes a long time to entrust your thoughts to someone else. But first things first: learn to seek help from those around; before you learn the hard way. Furthermore, you need to "accept the truth of the past." This is the key to emotional freedom. To put it in a more pronounced way, I would prefer we said, "making peace with the past."

There are wars we can never win, and there are situations we may never "undo." But it takes real courage to accept the losses and wins of life. Oh, did I forget to say Kimberly overcame her traumas? Yeah, she did surprisingly. It was tough, and it was not an easy sail, but she did anyway; because she asked for help. I want you to know that no one will run around offering you a helping hand—you ask for it. Remember, the mind is not a transparent glass. So, until you ask for help, no one would give it to you freely. Then what must you do? Ask, talk, and keep talking until you find that which would liberate you from the toxic emotion.

In addition to making peace with the past, one needs to "admit their fault."

Truthfully it can be a hard task to do because no one wants to take the blame for their wrongdoings. We think it is safer playing the victim to get more sympathy; that feeling can be overwhelming, yes, but that will only cause more harm than good. Recognizing one's fault in a failed relationship is not an easy decision to make. But it is a big step to freedom. We are imperfect, and we are humans and as such are bound to make mistakes.

Freedom

The word freedom has a wide range of meaning. For an inmate, freedom means to be released from prison. For a democratic country, it means an unconstrained way of talking or behaving as citizens. Nonetheless, for some it might be termed as "a light at the end of a tunnel." This five-letter word "light" has liberated many from seen and unseen dark moments. Just as breakups starts from the mind before it becomes a physical detachment, freedom also comes from ones thought.

To break free might seem impossible at the first but try and never stop. Scream and cry if there is a need to, but don't stop trying because negative emotional encapsulation can be deadly. Truthfully, humans can be selfish. But also, no one wants to have a feeling of guilt for not helping. So, my candid advice to you: seek help to gain your emotional freedom, because you cannot conquer the world alone.

Chapter 9:
The Power of Your Mind is Limitless

You are blessed with the most advanced and complex machinery that has ever existed—your mind. Man, out of all the living things on Earth, has an edge that goes beyond evolution: he has the power to create the world he desires. Just think it, and it will happen that house you've always envisioned for you and your family; that exotic vacation destination, a rich bank account. It's that simple. Even though we come across materials that tell us about the unlimited power of the mind, we have yet to grasp the true meaning of it. Perhaps, we may never get to truly understand how vast our minds are.

From the moment we are born, we are granted the ability to interact with our environment, and to form thoughts and perception based on our experiences. It is during these formative years that we learn from our parents, teachers, peers, and community. Sometimes, those who surround us unconsciously pass on and stamp their perception and beliefs about life. More so, we tend to create our perceptions based on these. Unfortunately, we create an unending circle of limitations.

Consequently, we feel powerless and live our lives on autopilot without a thought of breaking the self-inflicted barriers we've placed in our minds. Despite our extraordinary minds, we are depressed, disconnected, mentally unfit, and apathetic. Some can break free from these limitations and finally get to harness their potentials. These people are the ones you see as being blessed with everything you've ever desired for yourself. So, what sets you apart from those who seem to have it all?

Your Conscious Thoughts Set the Ball Rolling

Your answer lies in your conscious thought. Yes, your conscious thought is responsible for every decision you make, and this reflects in your subconscious which dictates your outcome. For instance, if you tell yourself, "I will win and be the best," you are conditioning your subconscious thoughts to align your outcome to that declaration. Therefore, if we don't have conscious control over our conscious thoughts, our lives will become like a ship without a rudder. Changing your conscious thought is a sure-fire to unlocking the vast potentials of your mind. Before we delve into how you can unlock your mind power, I'll like to explore the dangers of our reality.

Ironically, Reality Is A Blindfold

Let's be realistic; man cannot create machines for flying. Let's be realistic; it's impossible for a human to run 1000 miles in 11 days. Let's be realistic; there's no way a virtual currency can work. Yes, these are the words we hear every day. Perhaps, we say it quite a lot. Let's be realistic; I can't have that dream car with my salary. It's so easy to fall into the trap of reality. We mostly use it as a shield to protect us from experiencing hurt or disappointment. Over time, we've made it our defense mechanism. Unconsciously, these words have the power to limit your thinking power. No matter, how much you earn or try out different activities, you will never pass the limit of reality. Here's a question for you: have you ever seen any successful person utter those words? I'm sure the answer is no. Why? For you to break barriers and unlock your mind, you need to ignore the laws of reality. Reality will tell you that those who are born in a certain country or condition are prone to certain factors. More so, reality often works in conduction with research and statistics, to keep you under check.

People often see reality as their only truth. Well, this approach is wrong, as most people often associate reality with limitations and failure. I'm not disputing the fact that reality helps us to get in-tune with society. However, you should learn how to peer behind the curtains of reality, especially when it blocks your goals. Mind you, the only way you can accomplish that is to learn the art of positive thinking. Yes, positive thinking is a term we've come across in different motivational speeches and books. This concept is what you need to unlock the limitations of your mind. You might ask, "Why is it so important?" Not to worry, as we will explore this concept in the next section.

Positivity Is the Key to Unlocking Your Mind Power

I admit, maintaining a positive outlook is difficult for some, while it comes easily to others; it's a continuous struggle for some people due to constant life-changing circumstances. Therefore, you need to learn the art of positive thinking and how to integrate it into your conscious thought. By doing this, it will become a habit, hence impacting other aspects of your life. As mentioned earlier, positive thinking is a skill, and there are four stages you need to pass through before it becomes a habit. Personally, these stages have helped me to integrate and live positively even when faced with fierce challenges.

Hold on! You need to know that these stages that might not work for everyone who wants to learn positive thinking

You don't know how much power you have over your thoughts. This is a common problem with so many people: they find it difficult to see the world through another perspective. Their life experience has made them rigid; hence, pessimistic and unwilling to have a paradigm shift. When you realize that it is possible for you to learn positivity via a paradigm shift, then you are on the first step toward success. Acknowledge this fact, and let's move on to the next stage.

Positive thinking can be learned. More so, it can be cultivated until it becomes all you know. It's not enough to learn positive thinking; you need to know how to put it in action. No doubt, this is the hardest and perhaps the most exhausting stage. Why? Because it involves acting. Study people with a positive outlook on life, read books and materials on positive thinking. Never stop even when it's hard: your results are closer than you think.

When you reach this last stage, you have finally unlocked the power of positive thinking. This is the time when the act of thinking positively comes naturally, even when you don't feel positive. Although you might not feel positive all the time, your thoughts will always look for the good or silver lining in any situation. Just as the adage says, "you never forget how to ride a bike," if you practice more at positive thinking, it will become more of a habit.

To make positive thinking a habit, here a few ways you need to practice.

Start with Affirmations

Otherwise known as positive statements, these words have much more impact on your lives than you could ever imagine. Let's try out some positive affirmations:

"I am so grateful and happy for (fill in the blank space with whatever you are thankful for)."

Mind you, it doesn't matter how insignificant it seems. Here's another for you to try:

"It's so wonderful to (fill it with whatever you wish)."

Tell me how does it feel saying those affirmations aloud? More confident? Assured of a better tomorrow? Now imagine repeating it continuously until it becomes a habit. The truth is, most people unconsciously make negative affirmations about themselves or their circumstances in life. Gradually, we find ourselves going down the path of these negative statements. To avoid negative outcomes, we need to consciously make positive statements that works with positive emotions, such as being happy and grateful. Remember, it's more than saying these words; you must try and feel the emotion of the words.

Discard Pessimism and Embrace Optimism

Earlier, I explained the dangers of being realistic when optimism is needed. You need to have an optimistic view about life irrespective of your past or present circumstances. Ask yourself about the outcome you want. The outcome could relate to a goal in your life. Start by thinking of a positive income and expect the best no matter what.

Walk with The Right People

It is never too much to mention that you need to walk with the right set of people. I'm talking about those with a goal-getting mindset. According to philosopher John Rohm, "we are an average of those we spend the most time with." Here's something you might not have noticed: those you spend your time with have an impact on your emotions and thoughts. If you suddenly feel depressed, look at those who are by your side. There's a high chance your mood was triggered by something they said or did.

Be Grateful

Why should I be grateful when things don't play out the way I want? Well, you should know that there are many people who would give an arm and leg to be in your situation. Think you have it rough? Wait until you walk in another's shoes. Gratitude will help you to keep your mind on the positive, so you don't have time to think of the negatives in your life. It is not enough to say the words of gratitude; you must feel nervous before them. Confused on how to go about it? Here's a trick that has worked for me. Keep a gratitude journal. Try writing at least five things you feel grateful for and see how your attitude toward life changes.

Substitute "Have" With "Get"

Still having trouble with adopting a positive habit. Try substituting the word "have" with "get." Do you observe how many times we say we "have:" to do something? It happens all the time. I must write. I must complete this project. I must go to work. I must prepare the kids for school. Now change the word "have" to "get." I get to complete this project. I get to write; I get to go to work. Even, I get to pay my rent. What do you notice with this little change? Your attitude changes immediately from needing to fulfill obligations to being grateful for the things we've become accustomed to having: a roof over your head, kids, a job, a talent. Once you make this change, you will become happier, and it will unlock the limits you've placed on your mind.

Avoid Emotional Deadweight

Let's say your day was going well, but then you go to school or work and your colleague starts complaining about his life, job, or family. You didn't think about it before he/she brought it up. However, you find yourself agreeing and joining the bandwagon of complainants. Don't fall into the trap. According to research, complaining leads to depression, emotional and motivational deficits.

Take A Deep Breath

One of the reasons why yoga is so popular is because it offers us an outlet for our stress, frustrations, and negative emotions. What's more interesting is that breathing exercises are a core component of yoga practices. Your breathing is connected to your emotions. For instance, your breathing becomes fast and irregular if you have a panic attack. More so, your breath slows down when you are expecting or concentrating on something. Since you now understand the link between your breath and emotions, you can work toward controlling it.

Hold on To the Success Stories

Daily we hear stories of people losing their humanity, hunger, war, and natural disasters. It's difficult to have hope and stay positive when we hear such stories. However, we rarely see stories of people who rise during these trying times to make stronger change. Well, it's time to watch out for those success stories. Look out for the person who saved so many people during a natural disaster. Look out for those who fight against injustice, and there lies your beacon of positivity.

Make Others Smile

We mostly think of ourselves—yes, it's alright to take responsibility for ourselves. But set a target to make someone smile in a day. This time around, look outward instead of inward. Think about others' happiness, and this will help you to realize the impact of your attitude and expression on others.

Chapter 10:
Awaking the Giant when Defeated and Broken

We carry immense power within us. A power so great, it dwarfs our wildest imagination—it's limitless. We all have it. It's what makes us special in our way. The janitor at your office or school has it. Each of us has a unique power; your CEO has this immense power, even your colleagues have it. Now, here's a question: if we truly possess this immense power or giant within us, why are we in our current position? Why do we feel dejected and incapable if we have this immense power at our disposal?

Furthermore, if we have the same power as the elites, why are we not up there? Doesn't seem to add up, right? The answer is simple: we've simply lost sight of who we are. We have buried the giant within us underneath heaps and loads of worries, low self-esteem, our lackadaisical attitude, and in discipline. Our present condition has become our sole reality. Yes, we forget that we are so much more while we look on with envy at those who have awakened that power within them. Well, my dear reader, it's time. I know you are ready. The fact that you read this book to this stage means you are ready to cast off your old self and kickstart the process to awaken your power. In this chapter, you will not only learn how to awaken the giant within you, but how you create a compelling future for yourself and your loved ones. However, you need first to clear away the rubble that has buried your giant. Yes, you need first to learn how to believe in yourself.

Believe in Yourself

While growing up, some of our dreams were squashed by those who thought they were looking out for us. For instance, a child who shows an interest in drawing would be told about the financial hardship which befalls most artists. They take it a step further by saying that the child wouldn't achieve anything if he or she continues that path. Little by little, this unhealthy advice begins to chip away at the child's self-confidence in that skill and gradually spreads into other aspects of the child's life. Sadly, the voice never leaves even when we become adults and have families of our own. The voice taunts you when you summon the courage to start a goal. More so, it criticizes you when things get difficult and use it as proof of your incompetence. Yes, it's not easy to contain self-doubt since it sneaks up on you when you are unaware. Self-doubt is greedy and when let loose, devours our confidence and strips reason and logic from your mind. More so, it leaves you with fear and insecurity. Sometimes, you try to remove self-doubt with positive thinking, but it's not as effective as you might want. Here's what you've been doing wrong: self-doubt is not a depressing beast. Rather, it's a part of human nature, just like joy and happiness. You need to embrace self-doubt to believe in yourself. If you want to believe in yourself, you need to first identify your self-doubts. You can identify self-doubt when you utter sentences like, "I can't, "What if? "and "I have to..." Do away with such negative sentences and practice the following steps to believe in yourself.

Believe It's Possible

You will always have the nay-sayers around you: those who will tell you it's impossible. Don't listen to them. Rather, take hold of your mind and steer it to deliver the outcome you want. You just must discipline your mind to believe in possible expectations, and events will line up to give you that desired outcome.

Visualize Your Destination

Envision what your life would look like if you achieved your dreams. Remember, the mind is a powerful tool and motivator. By visualizing your destination, it will give you the needed to boost to reach your goal. You will notice you are unexpectedly doing tasks that move you closer to your dreams. You will find yourself volunteering to take on more responsibility, asking directly for what you want, taking the lead at board meetings, and eating healthy. Here's an effective way to carry out this step: I want you to create a visualization board. This is a graphic representation of your goals, and you can always go back to it when you feel less motivated.

Act as If You've Arrived at Your Destination

Let's say you dream of becoming a millionaire in the next few years. Ask yourself, "what type of friends would I keep when I become a millionaire? What about the clothes you would wear at that stage? Would you give a certain portion of your investment to charities or religious places?" One of the best and effective ways of establishing a successful mindset is to behave as if you are already the type of person who has achieved their goals. Whatever actions you identify, start doing them now.

Let's say you want to become a supermodel in the next five years. Start eating the type of strict diet you would eat when you finally become a supermodel. By doing this, you can condition your subconscious mind to find creative ways to achieve your goals.

Become the Best You Can Be

Once you are free from the depressing rubble of self-doubt, it's time to awaken that latent power within you. It's time to become the premium version of who you are. I want you to take into consideration that we have different perception about the best version of ourselves. Despite the difference in perception, one thing is common: your happiest version is the best version of yourself. Yes, happiness plays a huge part in this journey. No doubt, it is common to see many people belittle the significance of achieving their goals. I've seen so many people downplay the immense importance of happiness in attaining their goals. So, let's look at how to create your happiness since your best version is majorly dependent on it.

Creating Your Own Happiness

Who's in charge of your happiness? The answer is you. The choice to be happy or unhappy is the easiest thing in the world to accomplish. All you must do is decide. Have you ever wondered why children are the happiest? Their happiness stems from their inability to get weighed down by the circumstances of adulthood. If you ask a child what makes him/her happy, I'm sure they would talk about things we regard as mundane. For instance, they would talk about a fast train rushing by, streets lights shining on a river, a swallow flying, birds in the sky, and so much more. The kids can see the essence and wives/wonders of the world we live in. No doubt, to become happy you need to see through the eyes of children—without judgment. Happiness is achievable, but most people consciously and unconsciously manufacture their unhappiness. Although some unhappiness is caused by social conditions, these are of lesser proportion to that which we create by ourselves. Yes, most of our unhappiness comes from within, and it's time to let it go. You need to learn how to create your happiness to be the best version of yourself.

Our happiness majorly stems from cultivating the habit of the mind. In other words, cultivate the happiness habit, and your life will become a continuous feast. You can cultivate the happiness habit through positive thinking. It's quite straightforward, as we have discussed in the previous chapter. Create a mental list of happy thoughts and replay it in your mind every day. It's normally for a stray, unhappy thought to creep into your mind occasionally. When it does, substitute it with a happy thought.

Here's a lay-your-bed principle for happiness: every morning before rising, run a few happy thoughts through your mind. These happy thoughts will create a ripple effect that affects other habits and tasks for the day.

Know Who You Want to Be

Firstly, know the type of person you aspire to become. Create a list of the important qualities in your personality. Slow and regain your composure if you find yourself deviating from these important qualities. For instance, you want to become a happy person, come up with a plan to practice happiness even in stressful conditions.

Secondly, set achievable goals. Don't fall into the quagmire of setting unrealistic goals that will leave you frustrated and spent at the end. So, set specific and achievable goals which are easy to fulfill. In addition to this, you will feel good about them.

Thirdly, prepare for success. Always try to be one step ahead and eliminate things that might impede your progress. No doubt, being prepared will help you to feel less overwhelmed and stressed. At this point, do away with procrastination. Prepare for the next day's or week's tasks.

Lastly, surround yourself with energy boosters. Your energy boosters are those who support you and cheer you on with positive words. Don't spend time with toxic people. Furthermore, be a source of motivation and positive words to people.

Make Lifestyle Changes

Start by getting rid of the "junks" in your schedule, home, and life. It's just important to cut away the unnecessary parts of your life, to have an increased benefit in your specified area. If you have too much stuff or commitment, get rid of it. Since unnecessary things can cloud up your judgment, declutter your home, streamline your finances, and cut away unnecessary commitments.

Learn to say "no." We sometimes bite more than we can chew. It's alright to refuse some projects if you don't have the time to handle. Remember, it's better to say no than to perform below par on a project. Only include things you want to do in your priority list. More so, you can delegate tasks to others if your schedule is filled up.

Perform Self-Assessment. It's alright to gauge yourselves to see if you are still on the path of success or not through your thoughts and habits. Hold on! Don't judge yourself too harshly during self-assessment. Furthermore, create a plan to reduce your failures in the future.

Create a Plan to Achieve Your Goals. Most people don't think of the plan through which they will attain their goals. Start by dividing your goals into long-term or short-term. Create deadlines for these goals and formulate a plan to attain them. To help you fare better, use a daily planner to help allocate the time you need for each goal.

Invest in Yourself

It starts with you: everything you achieve starts with you. Therefore, it's only right to take care of yourself mentally and physically to achieve what you desire. Eat well, exercise regularly, get enough rest, and address your health issues immediately. Most importantly, your eight hours of sleep is important.

Create A "Me Time"

It's not selfish to dedicate a little time to a hobby; do something that you enjoy for yourself. Having me time will reenergize you and give you the energy to chase your goals.

Build Healthy Friendships

As mentioned in a previous chapter, you can't walk alone. Forming strong and healthy relationships will aid you to achieve your goals faster than when alone. Seek out for friends who accept you for who you are. Furthermore, build a friendship with those that model the qualities you desire.

Chapter 11:
Never Ring the Bell

There are moments in our lives where we feel all hope has been dashed out, and possibly, taking the next leap may be difficult. This situation happens a lot, and it can be very dramatic and traumatizing, I must confess. But it is necessary to have it in mind that many persons pass through this phase as they mature; so, luckily, you are not in this boat alone. Everyone at some point in their lives has felt the need to quit and run away even without trying. But did you know that many successful persons we know today, repeatedly tried without giving up? Yes, they never gave up. You need to see it as a motivating force. So, whenever this negative feeling of staying down creeps into you, brush it up, keep moving, and never quench the zeal to persevere. You know, it would sound unrealistic if a person told you they'd never had a challenge while growing up; of course, it's never been heard of and as far as I am concerned, it is unbelievable.

Nobody has it all and life isn't a bed of roses; even the kids born with the silver spoons can attest to that fact. So, if anyone ever told you there won't be struggles, challenges, setbacks, and failures, the person lied to you, and of course, you need to wake up from such dreams.

Furthermore, you need to know that the world is messed up and sincerely, everyone is struggling to make a life out of it. The topsy-turvy of life is a constant factor, and our fears and challenges are a sure thing. Also, facing short and long-term failures are all a part of growing up. But you would agree with me on this note that all situations in life have their seasons. Some may be unpleasant, yes, and others may be good. But, in as much as we have these feelings of fear and doubt, it is paramount to know that unpleasant situations are not a permanent phase in life. Although to some people, it might feel that their share of bad moments is much more than others, this in no way should deplete ones motivating force. And, it should for no reason turn you into a weakling or make you quit even before trying. It is just a phase, and you need to persevere whatever the cost may be.

So, What Is Perseverance?

Perseverance sometimes may be referred to as determination, courage, fearlessness, and endurance. Furthermore, it also can mean steady persistence in carrying out an action, purpose, or a dream despite the challenge faced. Having defined this term, I will give an example of someone who persevered.

You Owe Yourself A Breakthrough

Curt and Lewis were one of those kids in high school who knew what they wanted in life. Dreamers and writers—those were the right words to qualify them with. Their raw talents for writing were second to none. Curt's parents got him a tutor to polish him more with his writing skills. Lewis, on the other hand, had no one to put him through but himself and his mom. They both, in their ways, mastered the act since it was what they enjoyed doing. Most of their free times was devoted to writing and they improved each time they took the pen.

Interestingly, their family and friends were impressed with their growth because their stories were good enough to be published; but it never crossed their minds that someday, they could make a living from it. More so, the writing was what they did for leisure; it was never a chore. So, imagining their leisurely craft being published as a book was less thought to envisage. But a few years later, after graduation, they knew for a fact that their act could grow more than a hobby. So, they took a bold step and mailed some of their stories to a magazine, hoping it would be published. But sadly, it was rejected.

Unlike their friends and families who enjoyed reading their work, the magazine decided that their stories were crap and weren't worth reading. And so, they felt incapable and thought they could not write anymore. But to everyone's surprise, they wrote yet another story; and for the second time, it was rejected. These rejections consistently happened with three more attempts. You would agree it was spirit breaking, and of a truth it was. Who knows? Maybe you would also agree with the publishers that their first work was tacky. But then, one would also ask, "what happened to the rest of the stories they submitted?"

Were they not good enough to be published? Was it just a coincidence that all their works were rejected? Or maybe it was fate dealing with them? Sincerely, neither was the case here. The whole incident made Curt wallow in self-pity, and he concluded "it was fate" and probably, writing, after all, wasn't his gift; so, he stopped after the fifth time. But luckily for Lewis, his mindset was way different and he, however, continued writing and sent his new stories even upon rejection.

Interestingly, after a few years, he got a call from the same magazine, and that, I would say, was a breakthrough call. Of a truth, there were times Lewis almost gave up because it took almost forever to get the attention of the publisher. More so, there were moments he also thought it was best to quit. Nonetheless, he encouraged himself and persevered all through the difficult periods.

So, Be the Judge

Who amongst these two got better with writing? Who amongst them was given a chance? Who was ready to leap? Who gave up and who persevered? Lewis? Curt? Maybe I know your answers already.

Lewis got a response after years of perseverance and today, he has over a hundred books to his name. The truth in life is that people who keep trying, people who never quit, those who persevere at all odds, those who have vowed to never stay down no matter the rejection, no matter the number of times they are walked over, no matter the number of times they get a no; those I tell you, are the people who are likely to keep getting better opportunities in life. For a fact, the only obstacle to your breakthrough is you. You don't have to blame anyone else for the choices you make in life. No one promises a smooth ride; it is going to be a rough one, but no matter the number of times the vehicle stops, you need to take up the steering and zoom off.

Stop Making Excuses for Yourself

Excuses have become a syndrome to our daily lives; because the human brain is wired in such a way to give up easily, many people have become caught up in its web. Some individuals unconsciously see excuses as a trophy to be won and in fact, you'd find out that before any ideas are suggested to them, they are already giving a thousand and one reasons as to why it will not be successful. And the truth is, if maximum caution is not taken to this effect, these individuals will constantly see reasons to still be buried in their mess. Well, it is necessary to know that no blames are intended to these people. I have been among this category of persons, so I have a fair idea as to what extent the void may create. I often saw reasons why I couldn't continue with a pursuit anymore, and I gave excuses that were worthless. Most of the time, I drowned in my self-pity and blamed everyone else for it; it became a little difficult to break free. The truth is, everyone faces setbacks, but some have a way of turning it into a driving force. And others at the other hand see it as a point to stop; this attitude I will say would only lead to self-destruct. So, in as much as you want to be a success story to another person, it is necessary to pick up the broken pieces and save yourself from the dangers of staying down.

Decide and Achieve What You Want

Indisputably, no meaningful achievements have been accomplished without the topsy-turvy of life. It would shock you to know that most successful persons on Earth have passed through challenges that can ordinarily make a person question existence. And the truth is, we look up to these folks and want to achieve their successes. But we feel very reluctant to make the sacrifices they made; because everybody wants the easy bailout. If you care to know, nothing in life comes at the snap of a finger, you will, of course, pay some prices to achieve this feat. The price in this case is perseverance. More so, deciding the things you want to achieve in life will come with a lot of hiccups, but firstly, you need to take control of your happiness. This feeling has a way of making some persons achieve their daily goals. So, if you want to keep your decision and achievements alive, then you need to own it and do what makes you happy.

Prepare for Challenges

Well, setting new goals and starting them can be quite intriguing; actually, anyone can do it if they put their minds to it. But also, you would concur with me that apart from having ideas for a new project, there are other difficult tasks associated with achieving one's goal. Having great ideas is not a bad thing after all, but you need to be acquainted with the possibilities of failing. One needs to know and expect that challenges will surface; this knowledge of possible challenge would make you prepare ahead of time because no great achievement was ever accomplished without setbacks. So, if you don't want to quit after a few steps, then you need to be cautious of the fact that challenges are inevitable. For example, if I need to open an online store, I must make inquiries first about it. Of course, it would be unwise to jump into it because I have a dream of being an online store owner. So, to get me on track, I must seek enough counsel from established online store owners in order not to ruin the business even before it kicks off. More so, there would need to ask the question about challenges faced by online store owners; and these may include questions relating from poor website traffic, lack of capital, loyal customers, tax, inventory management, too many more. This, as you can see, would prepare me for any future occurrence and make me have an idea about subsequent challenge or failure in this line of work. So, in the long run, if I have the zeal to quit, I would strive to never give up.

Take the Bold Step

Fear is a factor on its own that negatively affects one's success. It makes a person frozen in their own time and for this reason, leads to unnecessary procrastination. You would be baffled to know that some dreams and great ideas have been sent to the abyss because of fear. But for a fact, I'd prefer I died to try rather than allow fear to prevent me from trying and achieving my goals. And of course, I've never in my lifetime heard about a person who was celebrated for not trying.

So, if you want to succeed in life, ask yourself tough questions as to why you cannot decide on a course of action. Asking these questions will not in any way harm you; the only thing it will do is help you filter your thoughts. So, peradventure the benefit of taking the first step outweighs your fears, then you are on the right part to the success, and in fact, you are good to go. In a nutshell, my advice to you is to never quit before trying, because you can only persevere when you take the first step.

Maintaining Focus

There are no shortcuts to great achievements. No successful person in history has taken the easy route; it is always a long path to success. Never giving up no matter the challenge has always been the way to go. And for a fact, if you need to maintain focus with a career or chosen field, you need to look past obstacles. You cannot persevere—much less be successful—if you forget the reason why you started. Of a truth, it is never an easy task. But it is necessary to occasionally look at the price tag as you accomplish your life goals. More so, maintaining focus would help you overcome any negative thought that would stand as a hindrance to achieving your set goals.

A befitting example would be that of a runner who sees the finish line and decides to get there. Truthfully, there may be side distractions to him finishing first; because our brains are finely attuned to see extreme agitation that diverts our attention. But you see, the price tag would be the only driving force that would push him to finish that race.

Furthermore, as an entrepreneur, maintaining focus can sometimes seem almost impossible because of some things you need to do; such as a continuous track of phone calls, emails, clients, and employees. So, in situations like this, having keen knowledge of your brains limitations and pushing past these limitations can enhance your focus and boost your productivity. Also, multitasking has been said to be another factor to losing focus. In as much as it is an important skill to our everyday lives, it also has a negative side which consequently reduces our intelligence to a certain percentage; dropping our brain power. Some research has shown that when we multitask, we get emotionally tensed up and make mistakes because of some we need to do all at once. So basically, the aim is not to constantly focus but to also have a bit of free time when multitasking. But all in all, when having this free time, make sure you don't drown excessively in it because it might shift your gaze. So, my advice to you; put on a positive mindset all the time and never lose focus.

Seek Help and Support

No one can achieve success alone. I am often amazed when people say they are self-made; it gives me chills because I know for sure that it is practically impossible. Sometimes, you may decide not to involve some persons to your plans, because of some reasons best known to you. But have it in mind, too, that some certain set of individuals— strangers, colleagues, chauffeur or even a cook—has a role to play either intentionally or unintentionally. So, for sure, everyone in their little ways contribute to a success story. Also, it is paramount to know that seeking help sometimes can be difficult; particularly when a person is in a state of dilemma.

Nonetheless, always solicit for support or help when you are in dire need of it. Furthermore, do not hesitate to dissociate yourself from people who are addicted to having a pessimistic view about success; because they will eventually leave you in the dark. One thing for sure is important here: when seeking help, get it from the right folks, get it from people who are more experienced in your chosen field of interest, and finally, get support from people who are happy to see you succeed—these are the people who will instigate that perseverance fervor into you.

Review Your Achievements and Failure

Before I go in-depth with this piece, I will like to give a quick description of what review means. According to several definitions, a review can be described as a critical evaluation or inspection for text or report; in other words, review may be referred to as an analysis of a piece of work. Interestingly, this word has saved many businesses, persons, and firms from the edge of collapse. You know, quite a few persons make great plans but most times, when these great ideas don't break through, then their world tends to be on a landslide; this is one of the reasons why a lot of individuals stay down after the first try. Well, it will interest you to know that one of the keys to being successful in life is reviewing and reevaluating set goals. So, if peradventure an idea fails, the best resurrection you could offer it is to review the patterns or steps you took at the first instance, and then try a different one. Furthermore, as failure is reviewed, success, on the other hand, needs to be reevaluated; because it would be a blow if after succeeding, one begins to retrogress. So, to achieve more in life, you need to constantly review, reevaluate, and most especially persevere through it all because your starting point to success is way beyond the sky.

Chapter 12:
Final Note

Congratulations on reading to the end. It was an eventful journey for both of us. For me, it's the fulfillment of a long-term goal: to write a book on money and success habits. On the other hand, it's a guideline for achieving your dreams, and an affirmation of your positive and negative actions in the journey of life. Yes, we have practically touched every aspect you need to know to tap into your inner giant. However, one part was omitted. Perhaps, I saved the best part for the last. Well, it's up to you, my dear reader, to decide if this part is truly the icing on the cake.

Your Goals Are Everything!

Yes, this is one part that was omitted. Although we explored this concept in different chapters, we only talked about specific areas that applied to the subject at hand. This time get ready to have an undiluted front seat to the word that has made giants out of small men. Before we delve into this amazing concept, I want you to read and follow this chapter actively rather than passively. Munch on it and incorporate it into everything you do. I'll advise you to read it repeatedly.

Goals are everything. Every achievement is a testament to the fulfillment of a goal. Look around you at the buildings, mega-corporations, and the little shops that dot your street; they are all the product of someone or a group of people's goals. Let's make it simple: look at your TV set, your smartphones, and laptops. All these objects were once ideas or dreams in someone's head. A century ago, no one would have believed that these objects would exist. There's more: the solution to some of our current challenges lies in someone's imagination right now. Some people's goals are just to pay their bills, to survive and have enough to get by, while some set giant goals to change their status quo. You should know that irrespective of your goals, you will never get to your destination if you don't take the step. Remember, all goal settings are followed by a plan formation and massive and consistent actions toward its fulfillment.

What's Stopping You from Setting Goals

We all have the power to act on your goals. The fact that we haven't been able to access the power is because we've failed to set goals that inspire us. So, what stops us from having a clear list of goals to improve mentally physically, financial, and emotionally? Is it the fear of disappointment? Some stopped setting goals because they failed to achieve them in the past, and they can't get over the fear of disappointment. On the other hand, some set goals and attach their happiness to goals that might be beyond their control. These set of folks may lack the flexibility to notice better and more worthy goals around them while moving in the direction of their goals.

We fail to realize that the process of setting goals works like our eyesight; the closer we get to our destination, the more clarity we gain, not only on the goal itself but on the details around the goal. Perhaps, you might prefer one of those other possibilities. As you read on, you will discover that pursuing your goals brings you closer to your life's true purpose.

The strength to chase your goals may come from life's many disappointments or the stark realization that life is passing you by. For others, inspiration is a source of motivation. Irrespective of your source of motivation, I would like to introduce you to the key to achieve your goals.

The Key to Achieving Your Goals

When you take the step to achieve your goals, you've acknowledged the desire that we all have for constant improvement. There's a power in being dissatisfied with your current situation. There's a power in the tension of temporary discomfort. This strength will help you to push on through the pain and the discouragement. To achieve your goals, you need a certain level of discomfort to motivate you to push forward and increase the quality of your life and those around you. Many people try to shy away from discomfort or pressure, yet it is the absence of pressure creates a sense of boredom and lackluster character toward life. Truthfully, we feel excited or alive when we feel pressure of discomfort within us. However, this is different when we are overwhelmed by pressure or tension. There's a difference between being overwhelmed by stress and being the master of stress. Therefore, become the master of stress and use it to move you in the direction you desire. More so, you could put yourself under stress by enlisting the help of those you respect to accomplish your goals. Simply announce before these people that you would do everything in your power to pursue your goals. So, whenever you want to quit, you would remember your public announcement and push on.

Live Life to The Fullest!

It's sad to see some putting off joy and happiness in the pursuit of their goals. They believe that they will truly become happy and enjoy life to the fullest once they achieve something. Well, here's the truth: you stand to achieve more when you are happy and joyful. Although goals give us a sense of direction, we must constantly strive to live each day to the fullest, with no compromise. Do not measure your failure or success in life by the accomplishment of each specific goal you set. Remember that the direction you are heading to is more important not the specific goals. Sometimes, you may never get to accomplish that goal. However, the fact that you are in the right direction is an advantage since you would meet other goals to achieve.

Create Your Future

Here's a question for you: what would you do if you knew you couldn't fail? As the thought runs in your mind, I want you to write it down. Don't bother with the specifics of the goals. Just write, "Picturesque recreation center, Bahamas" or "Dream House, Big Garden, Beverly Hills."—you will fill in the details later. Now, I want you to believe and have the assurance that you can attain these goals. Divide your goals into personal development goals, adventure goals, contribution goals, and business/career goals.

Your Personal Development Goals

These goals are centered on your physical, mental, and social development. In this section, write everything you would like to improve in your life about your personal growth. You might want to learn a new language or read 52 books in a year. In terms of emotional growth, ask yourself the self-inflicting patterns you want to break or the toxic relationship you want to quit. Perhaps, you want to learn how to feel compassion for those you abhor. Mind you, the secret is to keep on writing these goals without stopping. Write to them as they come to mind. It could be a short-term goal that you can accomplish within a week or month. Alternatively, it might be a long-term goal that takes years to achieve.

Once you've written down your goals, take a minute to add a timeline to each goal. Hold on! Don't get scared about how you are going to accomplish these goals—it's not important. Rather, I want you to set a timeframe for each goal. This will condition the subconscious and conscious to make those changes goals possible.

Choose your most important goal. Choose a goal that would give you much excitement and fulfillment if you achieved it within a year. Now take a few minutes to write a compelling paragraph on why you are committed to achieving this goal. Write down what you will gain by achieving it. Ask yourself, "What would I miss out on if I don't achieve it?" These are the reasons and questions you need to consider when you feel like giving up on your goals. Make these your driving force and you will achieve beyond your imagination.

Career Goals

In this section, write down your goals for your career, business, and financial status. Set a standard you want to meet. Once again, take a few minutes to pen out your goals. Just keep writing as it comes to mind. These goals could revolve around why you would like to become the leader in your company, your net worth at a certain age, your retirement age, and so many more you deem as important. Now, follow the same strategy as your personal development goals.

Achieving Your Goal Is Not the End

Most people have the misconception that achieving our goals is the end. We fail to realize that by pursuing our goals, we create a ripple effect that affects our environment. For instance, a businessman sets out with the goal to build a business and earn a profit. In the course of earning money, he/she creates jobs for people. More so, these folks, in turn, provided a livelihood for their family. Furthermore, the kids contribute by becoming doctors, lawyers or any professional and nonprofessional job. No doubt, it's an unending circle.

See your goals as a transport medium to a destination, and not as the end of the journey itself. Remember, your goals are the tool to help steer you in the right direction. More so, achieving your goals will never make you happy in the long-term. Rather, it's who you become that gives you long-term happiness.

Here's one more secret for you: never delay your goals. Once you write it, take the step immediately. You might not have the required motivation to tackle the task again. Start while it's still fresh in your mind. With this in-depth analysis, you can comfortably reach your goals.

If you find this book helpful in anyway a review to support my endeavors is much appreciated.

How To

Jeremy Clark

CPSIA information can be obtained
at www.ICGtesting.com
Printed in the USA
BVHW042014241119
564537BV00019B/265/P

9 781647 450199